The Culture of Conformism

The Culture of Conformism

Understanding Social Consent

Patrick Colm Hogan

Duke University Press   Durham and London 2001

© 2001 Duke University Press
All rights reserved
Printed in the United States of America on acid-free paper ∞
Typeset in Quadraat by Keystone Typesetting, Inc.
Library of Congress Cataloging-in-Publication Data appear
on the last printed page of this book.

To my nieces,
Erin, Maggie, and Maureen

CONTENTS

ACKNOWLEDGMENTS.   I am grateful to two anonymous referees and the members of the Duke University Press editorial board for their helpful comments on earlier versions of this manuscript, and to Jerry Phillips and Stanley Fish for their support of this project. I am indebted to Nicole Consentino, Rebecca Johns-Danes, Laura Sell, and Sharon Parks Torian of Duke University Press for their help and expert handling of the manuscript, and to Cindy Milstein for thoughtful copyediting. Most of all, I would like to thank Reynolds Smith for his careful reading of several versions of this manuscript, insightful criticism, and continuous help and encouragement.

Et personne ne se révolte.
Pourquoi? C'est incompréhensible.
—MOHAMMED DIB, *La grande maison*

The Culture of Conformism

Social Stratification and the New Conformism

Social critics and dissidents in the United States and elsewhere are perennially baffled by the pervasiveness and tenacity of social consent—not only the acquiescence of ordinary people in an unequal social and economic system but their positive support of and contribution to the maintenance and extension of that system. Why do so many people readily accept and even further a system that seems so unjust to many of us, and so unfair to the very people who support it? The answer is difficult, for the factors contributing to consent are complex. There is no one thing that explains conformity. People acquiesce in a current system—whatever it might be: feudal, capitalist, socialist, democratic, authoritarian, or whatever—due to a broad range of forces, beliefs, desires. Some of these are blatant; some are subtle, but mutually reinforcing and with great cumulative effect. Classical political science, especially historical materialism, has isolated many of these factors. Still, the prevalence of conformity remains troublesome—practically as well as intellectually.

Indeed, the problem is perhaps more pressing now than ever, for after the great upheavals of the 1960s, the United States has not witnessed a further expansion of robust individual liberty and collective equality. Rather, here and throughout much of the world, there has been an apparent retreat into forms of economic thought reminiscent of the period before the Great Depression and forms of social practice that many believed were left behind in the 1950s.

Of course, the most obvious response to the puzzle of social consent is simply to reverse the question: Why should people revolt? Life is good.

Things are going well. There is food, clothing, and shelter in abundance. People are prosperous and content. What could possibly motivate us to dissent?

The problem with this response is largely a matter of one word: *us*. Certainly, some people are doing quite well, and their consent to the current system is unproblematic. But are all or most people doing that well, so well that acquiescence in the current system is readily explained by their economic, social, and political flourishing? Consider the economy. Though economic data are never unequivocal, though they are invariably open to differing interpretations, they point to some serious problems with this rosy picture. According to Congressional Budget Office data, as analyzed by the Center on Budget and Policy Priorities, 20 percent of U.S. households receive over 50 percent of the national income (Johnston 1999, 16) and average almost four times the mean income of the remaining 80 percent (Bureau of the Census 1998). Moreover, as the effects of this are cumulative, these households control a still higher percentage of the national wealth. Drawing on the University of Michigan's Panel Study of Income Dynamics, "a widely cited continuous survey of household finances" (Bradsher 1996, 32), Keith Bradsher reports that by the mid-1990s, the richest 10 percent of the population held over two-thirds of the nation's wealth and had an average net worth of nearly $1.5 million. The poorest 20 percent had a negative net worth (that is, debts exceeding assets) of over $7,000 (31). In contrast, consider an egalitarian system wherein any 20 percent of the population would have 20 percent of the wealth.

By this standard, 80 percent of the population in the United States is currently receiving less than its equitable share of the national wealth.

In the current system, Bradsher continues, the "bottom" 60 percent has less than 6.5 percent of the country's wealth (31); it would, of course, have almost ten times that amount in an egalitarian system. By comparison, according to Isaac Shapiro and Robert Greenstein's 1999 analysis, the top 1 percent owns 40 percent of the wealth—over six times that owned by the bottom 60 percent of the population, and two and a half times that owned by the bottom 80 percent. Returning to the University of Michigan study, it is clear that even those in the 75–89 percentile range have slightly less wealth than they would given an equitable distribution, their actual share summing to less than 12 percent (Bradsher 1996, 31; it would, obviously, be 15 percent given equitable distribution). This indicates that the "break-even" range—occupied by those people whose current share of wealth is roughly what it would be in an egalitarian system—falls only in the second decile. Put differently, an equitable distribution of the country's wealth would greatly harm 10 percent of the population, leave another 10 percent relatively unaffected, and overwhelmingly benefit the remaining 80 percent. Unsurprisingly, it turns out that around 80 percent of the U.S. population "regard the economic system as 'inherently unfair' and the government 'run for the benefit of the few and the special interests, not the people'" (Chomsky 1995, 113).

Needless to say, the problem is not unique to the United States. The situation is only worse internationally. For example, UN Human Development Reports show that more than half the world's population has an income of less than $750 per annum (Crossette 1996, A3), and 1.3 billion people survive on half that, or less than $1 per day (Bleifuss 1999, 1). Correlatively, 358 ultrawealthy individuals "control assets greater than the combined annual incomes of countries with 45 percent of the world's people" (Crossette 1996). Referring to the 1999 UN Human Development Report (Jolly et al. 1999), Bleifuss (1999) points out that "the combined wealth of computer wizard Bill Gates ($90 billion), financier Warren Buffett ($36 billion) and Wal-Mart heir S. Robson Walton ($15 billion) totaled more than the combined gross national product of the world's 43 least-developed countries, which have 600 million citizens." In keeping with this, the report explains, "the fifth of the world's people living in the highest-income countries" had "86% of world GDP" (Gross Domestic Product), leaving 14 percent for the remaining four-fifths (Jolly et al. 1999, 3).

Returning to the United States, we find that the consequences of these inequalities are often devastating, sheer deprivation extending to basic human necessities for significant portions of the population. An editorial in the *Nation* observes that "according to the Census Bureau, one-quarter of all *full-time* workers make less than $17,000, which is $4,200 less than they need to 'afford' a typical two-bedroom unit" (Naked Cities 1997, 3). Meanwhile, "homeowners' deductions for mortgage interest and property taxes and capital gains exemptions for the sale of houses (most of which subsidies go to families making more than $75,000 a year) cost the government $100 billion in taxes—five times what it spends on low-income housing" (4). The resultant homelessness is hardly compensated by government programs; almost one-quarter of "requests for shelter . . . by families with children" are "turned down because of lack of capacity" (3). As Juliet Schor (1991) points out, "According to a 1989 Gallup Poll, 13 percent of those surveyed reported that there were times during the last year when they did not have enough money to buy food. Higher proportions (17 percent and 21 percent) did not have enough income for clothes and medical care. . . . And because the poll reaches only those with homes (and telephones), these numbers are understated" (114). Note that the economic improvement of the late 1990s only returned people to 1989 levels (see Bureau of the Census 1998, v; the Gallup Poll did not repeat this survey). In the somewhat worse conditions of 1992, the poll reported that 48 percent of the respondents were worried that they would "not be able to pay medical or health-care costs" in the next year (Gallup 1992, 14). The Census Bureau report "*Extended Measures of Well-Being: Meeting Basic Needs*," asserted that "in 1995, approximately 49 million people—about 1 person in 5—lived in a household that had . . . difficulty meeting basic needs," such as food (Bureau of the Census 1999, 1).

At least for the poorest segment of the population, the situation is likely to worsen, due to so-called welfare reform and the increasing economic polarization of society (on some results of welfare reform, see Primus et al. 1999; and Parrott 1998). A survey conducted by the National Governors' Association found that almost half the people "who left the welfare rolls did not have a job"; the majority of those who do get a job receive less than $7 per hour, "not enough to raise a family out of poverty" (Houppert 1999, 17). Before welfare reform, *Meeting Basic Needs* reports that "when asked about help they would receive" if in need, over 77 percent "said help would be available from some source" (Bureau of the Census 1999, 7). Yet, when people actually "experienced financial troubles, only 17.2% did receive help" (7). Much of that help was from governmental agencies or programs now being restricted, phased out, or defunded (8).

The situation is worsened by the disparities themselves. Recent studies indicate that inequality has direct and deleterious consequences for health, beyond the impact of deprivation alone. For example, average life expectancy appears to decrease as income distribution becomes more unequal. Indeed, drawing on data from the World Bank and elsewhere, Richard Wilkinson (1990), of the Trafford Centre for Medical Research at the University of Sussex, has argued that "income distribution is . . . probably the best single predictor of longevity among developed nations" (391; see also Hay 1995, 159 n. 59). Indeed, "equity is the key to the health of the nation as a whole" (408).

Part of this economic inequality results from the underemployment and unemployment, both of which have continuously been much higher than would occur given temporary shifts in labor. Even in periods of economic expansion, the number of unemployed, discouraged, and underemployed workers rarely drops below one in ten (for recent U.S. figures, totaling about 11 percent, see Jolly et al. 1999, 215)—and this is based on official calculations, which almost certainly underestimate the situation. Needless to say, these figures increase, sometimes dramatically, during periods of economic contraction. Unemployment is particularly devastating, even beyond straightforward economic need. As Joshua Cohen and Joel Rogers (1983) have pointed out, citing a Johns Hopkins University study among others, "Each percentage point increase in the unemployment rate is for example associated with 318 additional suicides, a 2 percent increase in the mortality rate, a 5–6 percent increase in homicides, a 5 percent rise in imprisonments, a 3–4 percent increase in first admissions to mental hospitals, and a 5–6 percent increase in infant mortality rates" (29).

The effects of inequity do not stop there. Economic stratification depresses the quality of life for all people in our society, not only those who are poor or unemployed. First, it appears to reduce the entire stock of wealth in a society. The pie is not just divided unfairly; it is smaller, and thus there is less available for fair or unfair distribution.

Of course, this runs contrary to received economic wisdom. Indeed, the obvious response to our quandary about the distribution of wealth is that inequality fosters excellence, which in turn produces economic growth, resulting in more wealth for everyone. In this trickle-down view, equitable distribution would result in less wealth even for the poor. But precisely the opposite appears to be the case. Robert Frank (1999), Goldwin Smith Professor of Economics, Ethics, and Public Policy at Cornell University, points out that a "burgeoning empirical literature has found a negative correlation between . . . income inequality and economic growth in cross-national data." For instance, one study found that "national income rates in 65 countries were negatively related to the share of national income going to the . . . top 20 percent of earners," while "larger shares for low- and middle-income groups were associated with higher rates of growth"

(243). In short, research suggests that *more* inequality means *less* growth, while *less* inequality means *more* growth, thus more total wealth for all.

Needless to say, the deleterious consequences of inequality are not confined to economics but broadly affect the quality of life, even, in some cases, for the wealthy. Consider crime—a constant cause of fear and inhibition throughout the country as well as across social classes. The award-winning criminologist Elliott Currie (1998) notes that "despite a recent downturn in the crime rate," the United States remains "the most violent advanced industrial society on earth," and "Americans continue to put violent crime at the top of their list of concerns" (3). The threat is related directly to the economic stratification just mentioned. Drawing on a wide range of national and international studies by researchers at Cambridge University, the University of Toronto, the University of California, and elsewhere (124–30), Currie argues that "the links between extreme deprivation, delinquency, and violence . . . are strong, consistent, and compelling" (131).

In fact, crime is not simply a matter of absolute economic well being ("extreme deprivation") but stratification itself. Basing his analysis on a historical study of England and North America over the last three centuries, Douglas Hay (1995) contends that crime rates are closely related to economic inequality. As a general rule, more inequality means more crime; less inequality means less crime. Hay traces a history of shifting crime rates and economic conditions from 1500 to the present, making a strong case that they are directly correlated (147–51, 157). A more technical study, published by the World Bank, reaches the same conclusion, using "information from the United Nations World Crime Surveys" on "crime rates for a large sample of countries for the period 1970–1994." Put simply, the "results show that increases in income inequality raise crime rates" (Fajnzylber, Lederman, and Loayza 1998, vii). The study's authors go on to urge "redistributive policies," and "equalizing training and earning opportunities across persons" (31). The various academic studies cited by Currie (124–34) lead to these conclusions as well.

Unsurprisingly in this context, the U.S. incarceration rate is staggering. In 1996, J. W. Mason reported that 1.5 million people were in prison, and "millions more" were "on probation and parole" (34). The Bureau of Justice Statistics (n.d.) puts the figure at 5.3 million convicted offenders under the jurisdiction of corrections agencies that year. Research from a few years earlier shows that "local law enforcement authorities kept more than 50 million criminal histories on file"—a number that has no doubt increased since that time (Mason, 34). According to Mason, "one in five Americans is officially a criminal" (34).

Economic inequality is politically disempowering as well. It is no exaggeration to say that the governmental structure in the United States and the individuals who have positions within it largely serve the interests of the opulent few. The most obvious way in which this occurs is through campaign financing and the funding of ballot initiatives. Robert McChesney (1999) observes that the reduction of representative democracy to a game manipulated by paid advertising—and thus, by those wealthy enough to pay for advertising—advanced significantly through commercial television, beginning in the 1950s (261). By the early 1970s, the results were clear, leading to the passage of the Federal Election Campaign Act of 1971 and its amendment in 1974 (which was partially overturned by a 1976 Supreme Court decision; see Mann forthcoming). These efforts had little positive impact. According to Cohen and Rogers (1983), "In 1978, the bigger spender in campaigns for either the House or Senate was the winner more than 80 percent of the time" (34). Corporations won a comparable percentage of ballot initiatives "in which their spending significantly exceeded the spending of their opponents" (35).

The trend did not end in the 1970s. Of course, not every election can be won simply by outspending one's opponent. As McChesney (1999) puts it (focusing on the late 1990s), the centrality of money in guiding elections "does not mean" that the bigger spender "will always win." But it does mean that "a candidate without a competitive amount of cash will almost always lose." Moreover, "candidates with the most money who run the most ads have the inside track to set the agendas for their races," for their advertisements will tend to determine what issues are discussed, and how they are framed (265).

It is already clear that this is undemocratic—but just how undemocratic? Just what portion of the citizenry does campaign money represent? McChesney explains that "in the United States the richest one-quarter of 1 percent of Americans make 80 percent of individual campaign contributions," thereby "purchas[ing] the allegiance of politicians who, when in office, pass laws that work to the benefit of the wealthy few" (261). In effect, the vast wealth of a tiny minority determines electoral politics. As

Skip Kaltenheuser (1997) argues, "Our system of campaign finance attacks the concept of one person one vote" (57).

That is not all. Government officials themselves are regularly drawn from the corporate elite, or enter its ranks after leaving office (see Anker, Seybold, and Schwartz 1987, 104–5; for a more detailed discussion of one administration, see Brownstein and Easton 1982). Furthermore, through government advisory committees and independent policy-formulation bodies, such as the Council on Foreign Relations and Committee for Economic Development, "business is able to structure the activities of government so that its interests are built into the policy-making process" (Schwartz 1987, 79; see also Anker, Seybold, and Schwartz 1987, 106–15). All this leaves the overwhelming majority of people with no significant voice in the formulation or execution of public policy.

It seems obvious, then, that our society is not structured for the benefit of the many but for the few; that it is neither just toward the collective nor advantageous for the individual. Eighty percent of the population suffers deprivation in the distribution of social goods. Only 10 percent substantially benefits from this inequality, and less than 1 percent appears to have a real say in governance.

Thus the quandary introduced earlier: why do people not rebel? Even more surprising, why do so many men and women actually oppose the ideas and actions that could give them the security they lack, the material and physical well-being and sense of community they desire? Once again, the problem seems even more pressing now than it was in earlier periods. In the 1960s, there were vibrant popular movements of rebellion against war, racism, sexism, and poverty. There were intense, consequential struggles against oppressive stratification in the United States and throughout the rest of the world. But in recent years, the entire range of political debate and action appears to have shifted dramatically toward the acceptance or even extension of stratification, toward social consent, toward conformism.

In the following pages, I examine the multiple, complex, and mutually reinforcing factors that give rise to consent. Needless to say, many of these factors have been isolated by earlier theorists. However, earlier treatments of consent have tended to be one-sided. Political and social treatments give short shrift to human psychology; psychological accounts reverse this bias. Indeed, even internally, these accounts are excessively limited. Classical marxist depictions of "repressive state apparatuses" stress the brute force that helps maintain any social hierarchy. Such accounts, however, rarely treat the detail and diversity of that force with analytic clarity. While they rightly point out that the police operate to protect capitalist relations of ownership, they rarely explore the degree to which such explicit, legal force is bound up with a broader system of coercion ranging from various forms of official intimidation to permitted levels of individual terrorism, the latter enabled by what might be called "oppressive corruption." Standard accounts often note that law itself is shaped by the interests of social hierarchy, but they less frequently examine the precise ways in which law creates discriminatory distinctions even in such seemingly straightforward matters as the definition of homicide.

Similarly, psychological work has tended to focus on psychoanalytic issues, largely ignoring the vast body of cognitive research that is potentially invaluable to an understanding of social consent. Social critics and theorists have thus given relatively little attention to the ways in which human cognitive processes—such as prototype-based thinking, or cognitive modeling from specified lexical domains—operate to foster conformity and acquiescence.

In the first chapter, then, I take up the issue of "rational" conformity, people's consent to the social system based on self-interest. This chapter begins with a look at formal coercion, examining the structures and practices just mentioned (policing, official intimidation, and so forth). It then turns to informal coercion, focusing primarily on the economy—both the large structures of stratification and more immediate, directly experiential structures of what I call "microhierarchization." Finally, chapter 1 considers the shaping of human aspirations by system-internal goals, and the production of "secondary gains" that tie a person's sense of well-being to a structure of local, limited privileges.

Chapter 2 turns to "internal coercion," exploring an apparently simple though in fact highly nuanced aspect of consensual ideology: belief. This chapter sets out some of the complexities of belief as well as systems of alternative beliefs or "problematics." It goes on to consider the ways in which beliefs are themselves hierarchized, analyzing the role of "meta-beliefs" and beliefs that bear on systems of expertise. In addition, chapter 2 draws on research in cognition, treating "fundamental beliefs"—which guide thought and action even when individuals have self-consciously repudiated them—along with such broad cognitive tendencies as "confirmatory bias" and "anchoring effect," which have strong consensual consequences.

The third chapter turns from belief to emotion. Drawing on social psychology, psychoanalysis, and cognitive science, this chapter focuses first on the formation of identity in relation to group definition, exploring the effects of this on narcissism, self-esteem, and empathy. People's views of their own positions in social hierarchies and their attitudes toward the positions of others—especially those who suffer more than they do—are inseparable from the identity categories in which individuals class themselves and the ways in which these identity categories operate. To further understand these categories, as well as other aspects of emotion and consent, I introduce several concepts from cognitive psychology, such as cognitive schemas and exemplum saliency. Finally, chapter 3 considers the more classical psychoanalytic topic of transference, partially reformulated in relation to cognitive structures and processes.

Chapter 4 takes up some further cognitive issues that are more removed from intuitive psychology, including prototype-based thought, lexical topicalization, and modeling based on cognitive domains. While earlier chapters drew on a range of political topics, this chapter focuses on one: racism and related forms of prejudice, such as homophobia. As many writers have noted, racism—or more generally, status hierarchization—is among the most divisive elements in society, not only in the United States but throughout the world. In its various forms, a bias of this sort operates to fragment classes of people who might otherwise join together for common betterment. As such, it is one of the most powerful forces for consent and conformity. The cognitive structure of racism, however, has been little understood. In this final chapter, I concentrate on this singularly important topic.

Finally, in a brief afterword, I present a few suggestions for those who are interested in following up their reading with positive action against some of the unfairness and inhumanity detailed in the preceding pages.

My first goal in this study has been to articulate an intellectually clear and practically useful account of what might be called "the new conformism": a culture of consent that has developed recently in this country. Yet, at the same time, I have sought to articulate a description of acquiescence in oppressive practices and structures that is of more general applicability as well—an account that is broad enough to clarify the structures of consent that operated in earlier periods and those structures that will continue to be crucial when the current phase of intensified conformism passes. In keeping with this, I have not confined my attention to the past decade or so (the period most obviously marked by the new conformism) but have drawn on events, conditions, writings, and so on from different countries and times in the past century, occasionally even earlier. Moreover, when I have turned to earlier decades, I have most often been interested in their connection with, not their difference from, the present. In short, this is a study of the modes of action and thought that constitute social consent, modes of action and thought that may be particularly pervasive now, but are continuous with what went before; it is not a history of variations in the flourishing and waning of consent.

This is also not a study of why people resist or rebel. There are complex and subtle patterns to rebellion, just as there are to conformity. The conditions that give rise to social movements, the strategies that most effectively spur political change, cannot be treated adequately here. They are the topic of another book. The two projects—that accounting for consent and that accounting for rebellion—are of course not unrelated, for rebellion arises precisely in conditions that operate to weaken or limit consent.

This relation leads to a practical point. The analysis of structures fostering consent is, by its nature, a project that paints a somewhat grim picture of human society and the human mind, a picture that may make one wonder how conformism can be limited at all, how rebellion against unjust stratification can ever be fostered. But the very same cognitive and affective structures that lead to conformity today may advance the cause of resistance and human decency tomorrow, through continuing struggles to change the conditions in which those structures operate. Consider a simple example. As I shall discuss in chapter 2, the recent rise in conformism is partly a media creation. Dissent is consistently underreported or even unreported, and when reported, it is misrepresented and diminished. One general principle of consent is that claims about conformity are self-fulfilling. A widespread belief that there is no dissent regarding a given policy or practice tends, in and of itself, to undermine dissent. In other words, the media fabrication of conformism tends to produce precisely that conformism; the appearance gives rise to the fact. Yet this same principle entails that a more inclusive representation of dissent in this society—

the more general exposure of nonconsensual, nonconformist actions and ideas—will itself foster dissent, will itself serve to pull against conformity.

In fact, there are hopeful signs of development in this direction—the founding of left-wing, but nonauthoritarian political parties, such as the Green Party, Labor Party, and New Party, the redevelopment of college activism, through such groups as the Center for Campus Organizing, and so on. (For the addresses of these and related organizations, see the afterword.) Moreover, historical patterns indicate that the current phase of hyper-conformism is likely to wane over the coming years, perhaps to be replaced by a new period of rebellion. Indeed, a particularly remarkable and heartening development has been the series of protests against globalization and related issues in Seattle, Washington, Philadelphia, and Los Angeles. These protests began only weeks after I completed what I thought would be the final version of this introduction. Perhaps they are the first sign that our current hyperconformism is nearing its end.

On the other hand, it is important to recall that rebellion, assuming it does develop from these hopeful beginnings, is likely to be warped by conformist ideas and practices, and be continually at risk of succumbing to those ideas and practices. The structures that foster consent do not disappear in periods of rebellion. They continue to operate, if less overtly, constraining that rebellion, and quite likely, eventually working to undermine it—thereby returning society, repeatedly, to a new conformism. In that sense, the new conformism is not something specific to the United States at present. It is a recurrent problem, a recurrent stifling of rebellion, resistance, dissent.

Ultimately, the primary value of a critical analysis of contemporary society is the degree to which it helps activists become more productive and effective in the pursuit of social justice—during periods both of conformism and rebellion; the degree to which it helps people respond to the current new conformism, and work against the development of other new conformisms in the future. My hope is that the following analyses will not only be of interest to those who wish to understand contemporary society but that they will also be of at least some practical value for those who have undertaken the long, tedious, unrewarding labor of trying to change that society.

ONE   *Rational Acquiescence:*

The Police and the Marketplace

The most obvious reason not to rebel is the power of the state and ruling classes. The use of coercion and threats of violence is most blatant in totalitarian countries, such as Indonesia or Guatemala over the last few decades. Yet it is centrally important in democratic societies as well. This is the first part of "rational" acquiescence: consent to the status quo based on an understanding of the physical, economic, or emotional harm one might suffer for rebellion. On the other hand, not all self-interests relevant to consent are coercive. Many concern positive goals, such as acquisition or advantage. This is the second component of rational acquiescence or, equivalently, "calculated consent": consent as a sort of structuring of human impulse, its limitation to certain objects and outlets.

LAW AND THE POLICE

Any legal system—with its police enforcement as well as penal codes and practices—functions in large part to preserve the social relations that define the society in which they operate. This preservative function includes the economy. The legal system places a huge repressive apparatus at the service of that structure. Douglas Hay (1995) presents some striking illustrations of this from the early nineteenth century. For example, "judges in all the common law countries" in this period insisted that "the injured worker should be almost always barred . . . from suing the employer, and that the family of the dead worker should be similarly barred from legal recompense" (144). The point is generalizable. All legal systems serve to sustain relations of ownership.

This may seem innocuous. After all, who wants their home burglarized? Who does not want protection against mugging? The specific way in which the legal system defines, say, theft, the way it categorizes and punishes crimes of property, is not a simple matter of evenhanded justice, however. It is a matter of preserving inequality. Consider the legal system in the United States (which does not differ significantly from other legal systems in this respect). First of all, it does not define ownership in terms of the production of wealth. Whether or not one accepts Marx's theory of value (I myself do not), it is clear that social wealth is created by the coordinated activities of all working members of society. One could imagine a definition of ownership according to which all individuals own that portion of social wealth that they have produced. Correlatively, one can envision a definition of theft according to which any appropriation of more wealth than one has produced is theft. As such, if the CEO of a factory takes 420 times the salary of a line worker (see "Everyone's Rich" 1999, 4), he or she is guilty of theft. (It is, of course, difficult to quantify the production of wealth. Nevertheless, it is hard to imagine an argument that, in one day, the CEO's work produces goods and services for society that are equivalent to the goods and services produced by a line worker cumulatively over an entire year and eight months. Indeed, many would contend that the CEO's contribution to the production of goods and services is *far less* than that of the worker, since most of the CEO's efforts are put into increasing profits for management and shareholders—thus in distributing social wealth, rather than creating it.)

But the present system is precisely the opposite of one that defines ownership and theft in terms of the production of wealth. It serves to protect the "right" of the CEO to appropriate and retain hundreds of thousands of dollars more than the line worker every year, to accumulate that wealth, and to increase it through investment. The worker's relation to his or her own production of wealth is not even a concept in the U.S. legal system (or in any other legal system with which I am familiar). In contrast, consider one of these line workers, who is unable to accumulate any wealth and may well lack adequate money to buy necessities for his or her family, or some unemployed person, fired from that factory due to a "downsizing" that increased the already bloated salary of the CEO. If one of these desperate and deprived people were to steal the CEO's wallet and get away with

$100, he or she would be guilty of grand larceny, and if caught and convicted, subjected to imprisonment.

Put differently, definitions of ownership and theft tend to be thought of as straightforward, even natural. But they are not. They are, rather, the product of human decision. That decision operates to give special protection to just those types of ownership (or putative ownership) that are crucial to economic stratification. It excludes from protection—or even from clear conceptualization—those types of ownership that would undermine or at least limit economic stratification. Indeed, this was the more or less explicit intent of the framers of the U.S. Constitution. As Noam Chomsky and others have discussed, James Madison viewed the property rights of the "opulent minority" as threatened by the masses, and thus as requiring particularly stringent protection. "To ensure that the rights of the opulent minority are privileged, they must hold the reins of government, Madison held. He added that this is only fair, because property 'chiefly bears the burden of government', and 'In a certain sense the Country may be said to belong'" to the propertied elite (Chomsky 1995, 118).

This is not to say that there are no laws restricting the acquisitiveness of, say, the business elite. There are. The legal definition of theft would be incoherent if it did not include various "white-collar" crimes. These are treated lightly, however, relative to their "blue-collar" counterparts—despite the fact that they are far more significant and consequential, even by the limited definition of theft. As Russell Mokhiber (1996) has noted, "Inside-the-Beltway corporate liberals and conservatives alike insist that crime in America is committed primarily by the poor and blacks," even though "corporate crime and violence inflict far more damage on society than all street crime combined" (14). Specifically, according to the FBI, "burglary and robbery combined cost the nation about $4 billion in 1995. In contrast, white-collar fraud, generally committed by . . . people of means . . . costs an estimated 50 times as much—$200 billion a year" (ibid.). Indeed, the systematic crimes of the elite are not even counted as such; the FBI "Crime in the United States report . . . documents . . . street crimes," but "ignores corporate and white-collar crimes such as pollution, procurement fraud, financial fraud, public corruption and occupational homicide" (ibid.).

As this last quotation indicates, the operation of law to coerce consent is by no means confined to property law. The most obvious cases are overtly prejudicial laws—laws that restrict voting rights to men, or laws that outlaw certain cultural, religious, or sexual practices. The latter guarantee that members of outlawed groups will be forced to conceal their identities, and thus prevented from engaging in public acts of solidarity and political agitation. Consider, for instance, laws discriminating against gays and lesbians. In the first chapter of *Sexual Orientation: A Human Right*, Eric Heinze (1995) gives a sampling of such laws from around the world. Iran executes "citizens who engage in private, adult, mutually consensual, homosexual acts," and those convicted of such acts have no right of appeal (3). In countries from Romania and Lithuania to Australia and England, people can be arrested for homosexual practices. Indeed, in the United Kingdom, "men who commit consenting homosexual acts are four times more likely to be convicted than men who commit heterosexual and violent offenses" (Peter Tatchell, quoted in Heinze 1995, 6). Moreover, a British court judged that it was within the law to dismiss a gay man from his job as a "means of assuring that he would not sexually harass customers" (6).

This bias toward preserving stratification spreads throughout the legal system. It is not only the legal definition of theft but those of assault, rape, spousal abuse, fraud, homicide, and other crimes as well that appear natural and neutral, even though they are, in fact, artificial and severely biased. Consider homicide. What could be more "natural" than to outlaw the taking of human life? True. The taking of human life, however, is not outlawed. Rather, what might be called "direct killing" is declared the monopoly of the state, with very limited exceptions. Just as with theft, small-scale street homicide, primarily perpetrated by the miserable and impoverished, is severely prosecuted, while large-scale elite homicide is generally permitted. Mokhiber explains that according to the FBI, the United States has a street homicide rate of "about 24,000 a year." These killings are felonies. First of all, the state can, at least in some cases, kill those judged guilty of these murders. More important, the state can kill many times that number of people—many times that number of civilians— in military conflict. Hence, during the brief period of the Gulf War, the state was able to kill Iraqi civilians at roughly eighteen times this rate, doing in "more than 50,000" (Clark 1992, 130) in only six weeks. (This does not count the hundreds of thousands of indirect deaths caused by the war [see Crossette 1995, A9; and Halliday 1999, 26] or the hundreds of thousands of Iraqi soldiers killed [Clark 1992, 43].) Clearly, this killing was not outlawed.

Legal definitions, such as that regarding murder, have two sorts of consensual consequences: they allow for a range of repressive actions, the threat of which fosters consent; and they tend to guide an individual's own thought as to what constitutes murder. Thus, most people unreflectively count street crimes, but not state-sponsored bombings, as murders. Indeed, legal definitions come to seem so natural that it is sometimes difficult to see that they are the product of choices, and choices with systematic social results. For example, murder is not consistently defined as the killing of innocent people, for then the massive killing of Iraqi civilians—men, women, and children who had nothing to do with the invasion of Kuwait—would have counted as murder. In a remarkable illustration of the consensual effects produced by such legal definitions, one colleague of mine, on reading the last paragraph, commented that only a "far far far Left ideologue" would class the bombing of Iraq as involving "murder."

This state monopoly on direct killing is not the only aspect of homicide law that is artificial and biased. Consider indirect killing (for instance, the creation of hazardous conditions that result in predictable deaths). Indirect killings in this country far exceed direct ones, and the perpetrators are overwhelmingly corporate. The Labor Department "reports that . . . 56,000 Americans"—well over twice the number killed in street homicides—"die every year on the job or from occupational diseases such as black lung, brown lung, asbestos and various occupationally induced cancers" (Mokhiber 1996, 14). Of course, much of this is supposedly covered by criminal law. But these sorts of indirect killings do not have anything like comparable legal status with street homicide. Again, suppose a worker is "let go" by his or her employer due to so-called downsizing, with the CEO increasing an already enormous salary. Suppose that this unemployed worker then goes and shoots this CEO. That is first-degree murder and can be punished by execution. Now imagine another scenario. The CEO is warned that the handling of certain chemicals may be dangerous to workers, but that a safer procedure would eat into the company's profits. The CEO decides to do nothing. There is an accident and four workers die. This is not first-degree murder and could never result in execution. Moreover, it is unlikely that anyone would ever be prosecuted for this crime. "Corporate violence that results in worker deaths rarely provokes criminal prosecutions. . . .

The National Safety Council estimates that since the passage of the Occupational Safety and Health Act (OSHAct) in 1970, 250,000 workers have died on the job," but "only four people have done time for OSHAct violations" (Mokhiber 1996, 15).

There are other biases hidden here as well—biases that become obvious after only the briefest reflection. If a street thug pulls out a knife and tells a passerby to hand over five dollars, he or she has committed a serious crime. The mere threat of the knife is prosecutable as assault with a dangerous weapon. Yet, if an employer tells a worker that he or she must handle dangerous radioactive chemicals or lose his or her job, that has no comparable status.

This is only part of the problem with legal definitions of murder. Corporations kill not only workers but consumers—and they often do so with full knowledge. The most obvious case of this is the tobacco industry, which is responsible for perhaps twenty times more deaths every year than street homicide. (Deaths from smoking have been estimated at between 400,000 and 500,000 [see Kluger 1996, 703].) Moreover, it is guilty of a theft of staggering proportions. In order to make profits on the sales of cigarettes, the tobacco industry has created a health crisis that drains perhaps $50–65 billion from national wealth. (On some complications with estimating these costs, see Kluger 1996, 553–54, 735–36.) Recall that burglary and robbery combined cost the nation only about $4 billion per year (Mokhiber 1996, 14). This economic cost is probably the reason that there have been a few successful civil cases against tobacco companies in recent years. These are certainly important, but even if they continue, it is clear that the tobacco industry is vastly underprosecuted and undercriminalized relative to street crime, which again, is far less harmful.

The tobacco industry is not the exception here but the rule. Note, for example, the fact that "for more than 20 years, the auto industry . . . defeated efforts to enact a federal law that would require air bags as standard equipment on all U.S. cars" (Mokhiber 1996, 15). The result of this is death: "Auto safety expert Byron Bloch . . . estimates that as many as 140,000 Americans . . . have died in auto crashes since the early 1970s because the auto companies' legislative privilege effectively thwarted all efforts to develop and legally mandate the device in American cars" (15). Clearly, the automobile industry's opposition to the law was the result of economic interest, which is to say the desire of owners and managers to acquire a higher percentage of the national wealth. Their motivation, in other words, was much the same as that of the street thug who shoots someone to steal his or her money. But there are two differences. No street thugs kill anywhere near the number of people killed by even one major automobile manufacturer. And street thugs typically begin with only a small fraction of their equitable share of social wealth, while CEOs typically begin with many, many times their share. Again, legal definitions of crime operate to perpetuate that inequity, and they lead people to think of that inequity as fair, rather than the result of theft and murder.

Beyond this, a great deal of corporate crime is subjected to civil prosecution only. This gives wealthy individuals and corporations an enormous advantage, for they have the resources to pursue civil actions against others or fight civil actions taken against them. This is untrue of the great majority of the population—those people who receive less than an equitable share of social goods. These individuals are rarely in a position to pursue litigation, no matter what has happened to them. In effect, the possibility of refusing consent through legal action is denied to them. This is still more obviously the case when their opponents are fabulously wealthy.

As this indicates, there is a broad bias in the procedural structure of the law. The prosecution of criminal law allows considerable advantages to the wealthy. The more money a defendant has, the more he or she is able to procure the most effective legal defense team. Conversely, the less money one has, the more likely it is that one will receive marginal or even incompetent counsel (for some shocking cases in death penalty trials—cases where poor people have been sentenced to death largely because of the stupidity and indifference of their lawyers—see Shapiro 1997). The entire structure of legal proceedings is organized in such a way as to maximize the advantages of the opulent minority. One can see this quite clearly by contrasting a system in which, for example, all criminal cases are handled by state prosecutors and public defense attorneys.

These discrepancies are only multiplied in civil law, especially when the conflict is between the wealthy and poor. Indeed, for the very poor, the only options for civil litigation against corporate malfeasance are, most often, via legal aid services, primarily through class action suits. It is almost always impossible for a poor worker to pursue an employer on his or her own. By joining other workers in the same situation, however, with the case pursued by legal aid services, such a worker can at least hope for a fair judgment—though even here he or she remains at a considerable disadvantage. This is why the extremely right-wing 104th Congress sought "reform" in this area. By outlawing the pursuit of class action suits by federally funded legal aid services—even when those suits do not use any federal funds (see A Promising Victory 1997, A16)—Congress undermined one of the few means by which the poor in this country could hope to achieve some sort of legal equality with the rich.

Moreover, everyone is aware of these constraints, at least in general terms. On the one hand, the legal system is a vast mystery for most people. Many do not understand laws, legal proceedings, or the court structure—not because people lack intelligence but because there is virtually no context in which they might learn any of these things. Nonetheless, one thing they do know is that any sort of legal action is likely to cost them large sums of money; that an action against a corporation or any member of the opulent minority is likely to be defeated by the latter's far more extensive resources—resources for hiring lawyers, researchers, favorable "expert" testimony, and so on. In short, for the miserable many, any attempt to pursue one's legal rights is at best a gamble: whatever the merits of one's case, one is likely to lose a great deal, both materially and emotionally, and gain nothing. The consensual effects of this are too obvious to require elaboration.

A further area of coercive possibility in law derives from the inevitable intervention of human judgment in legal processes. Laws do not operate autonomously; they are mediated by judges, juries, and police. Consider, for example, the enormous discrepancies in the sentencing of whites and blacks for comparable crimes. According to the *New York Times*, "A study by the New York Division of Criminal Justice Services . . . finds that members of minority groups are substantially more likely than whites to be jailed—even when they commit the same crimes and have similar criminal histories." In New York State, this leads to the incarceration of more than 4,000 "African-Americans and Latinos . . . for crimes and circumstances that do not lead to jail terms for whites" (Unequal 1996, A14; Clifford Levy [1996] indicates that the figure is about 4,300—roughly a dozen people *every day* who would not go to prison if they were white). Earlier studies found much the same pattern in other states (see Nickerson, Mayo, and Smith 1986, 260). These discrepancies are worsened by the fact that blacks are far more likely to be arrested for any given crime than are whites (see ibid., 261). For instance, J. W. Mason (1996) points out that "blacks . . . are arrested . . . at far greater rates than whites for drug crimes." And yet, "according to the U.S. Substance Abuse and Mental Health Services Administration, whites are in fact slightly more likely to be drug users" (36).

This is bad enough on its own. But it has further ramifications. These sorts of discrepancies not only foster fear, and thus consent; they contribute to political disenfranchisement as well. According to an editorial in the *Nation*, "Nearly 1.5 million black men—one in seven—are currently denied the right to vote because they are in prison, on probation or parole or have been convicted of a felony" (One in Seven 1997).

Finally, there are the police themselves. Even the most benevolent officials charged with law enforcement operate to intimidate the general populace, and thus to discourage any sort of behavior that might draw police attention. The situation is only worse when the officials appear to feel little constraint in the use of violence. Some commentators viewed the partial conviction of officers in the second Rodney King trial as indicating that there are significant, operative constraints on police violence. But, in fact, the Rodney King case reveals precisely the opposite. The partial convictions came about only because the brutality was caught on camera and because there was public outrage after the initial trial, leading to a second one. The Rodney King case made it perfectly clear, especially to African American men, that the constraints on police violence are weak. The case graphically told them: Physical brutalization is all you can expect from the police. Nobody will help you, and nobody will criticize the police, unless you have the good fortune to have every detail of the brutality recorded on videotape.

The Amadou Diallo case made the threat still more extreme and paralyzing. Worse still, the case was not some anomaly. "The police are using deadly force more and more frequently these days—and getting away with it," observes Salim Muwakkil (1997, 16). Amnesty International's "Police Brutality and Excessive Force in the New York City Police Department" clearly supports Muwakkil's view. This report points out that there were more than 2,000 charges of police brutality in New York in 1994. Moreover, there was a death in police custody roughly every other week. Indeed, "Amnesty International concluded that excessive use of force has probably led to many more deaths in police custody than the New York Police Department is willing to acknowledge" (Muwakkil 1997, 18). Amnesty issued similar reports on Chicago, Washington, D.C., and Los Angeles police. In

1999 news releases, Amnesty added to these criticisms, stating that "un-justified police shootings, excessive use of force, misuse of police dogs and harassment, continue across the country with alarming regularity" (1999b), and "in U.S. prisons and jails, physical and sexual abuse are endemic. . . . Inquiries into police brutality . . . show a pattern of systemic abuses" (1999a, 2).

The situation is only worsened by the increasing development of "para-military policing." Christian Parenti (1999) recounts the following scene: "Three squads of ten . . . officers in combat boots, black jumpsuits, mili-tary helmets and bulletproof vests lock and load their Heckler and Koch MP–54 submachine guns (the same weapons used by the elite Navy SEALs) and fan out through the neighborhood." He explains that the troops busy themselves "swooping down on corners and forcing pedestrians to the ground, searching them, running warrant checks, taking photos and en-tering all the new 'intelligence' into a state database." As it turns out, "All the suspects are black, all the cops are white." This is not apartheid South Africa but Fresno, California. Fresno is not unique. The United States "has more than 30,000 such heavily armed, militarily trained police units" (16).

Note that this sort of threat probably does not discourage people from murder or theft; indeed, as Joseph Dillon Davey (1998, 105–9) and others have discussed, even recent extensions of systematic judicial punishments, such as increased imprisonment, have only slight effects on crime. Rather, such a threat discourages people—especially minorities, who are the most common victims of this abuse (see Amnesty International 1996a, 1999b, 1996b)—from doing anything that might make them stand out, that might lead to an encounter with the police, and thus to the sorts of situation in which brutality and deadly force might be used. It leads, in short, to consent.

OFFICIAL INTIMIDATION, TERRORISM, AND
OPPRESSIVE CORRUPTION

Of course, policing and legal procedures are not the only means of system-atic coercion in capitalist democracies. Governments have a wide range of powers of intimidation that they can and do employ in special circum-stances. There were some striking cases of this during the assault on Iraq by the United States. For example, before the war began, the U.S. govern-ment engaged in a systematic campaign to intimidate reporters into leaving Baghdad. As Alexander Cockburn (1992) reported in the *Nation*, the U.S. press corps received "daily briefings from Joe Wilson, the U.S. charge d'affaires, telling them that if they stayed they would end up as 'ground round in a hole in the ground.' In the end Wilson chartered a plane and urged all Americans to leave."

The war itself had a powerful coercive effect on nonaligned Third World countries. The massive U.S. firepower, the brutal display of military superiority, was partly designed to be intimidating. As Middle East Watch observed in *Needless Deaths in the Gulf War*, the U.S. bombardment resulted in "the destruction of Iraq's electrical system, communications facilities, factories, railroads, waterways, bridges, and highways—in fact, the entire infrastructure," leading to "a public health catastrophe" that was "near apocalyptic" (summarized and quoted in Draper 1992). This is a frightening example for any Third World country that might defy the United States.

Returning to the home population, the most evident forms of coercion are often aimed at noncitizens. During the Gulf War, many European countries detained and/or deported resident Arabs (see Neier 1991, 295; and Lowe 1991, 14). In addition, many Arabs were listed as security threats—roughly 10,000 in Germany and Spain alone—often with "their names . . . on computer files across Europe, with state security forces closely cooperating" (Lowe 1991). In Germany, in a xenophobic action reminiscent of Nazism, "doctors, lawyers and public officials [were] required to hand over to the government all information they [held] on immigrants" (ibid.).

Ethnic minorities are also regularly subjected to direct and indirect government intimidation. During the Gulf crisis, the FBI visited hundreds of Arab Americans, in part to ask if they had information about terrorists. As Beth Stephens (1991) wrote at the time, "Questions have been as specific as to ask about the person's views on Bush's policy and on Israel, as well as for information about the individual's political activities." As a result, members of "the Arab-American community . . . are afraid to attend community events and are terrified of voicing any opposition to the war in the Gulf." Furthermore, during a state of national emergency, such as that declared by George Bush on 2 August 1990, the president has "the power to order 'the relocation of large numbers of people' " (Kraft 1991, 11), thereby potentially allowing the U.S. government to imprison Arab Americans much as it did Japanese Americans during the Second World War.

According to "Harper's Index," roughly one-quarter of the U.S. populace thought antiwar demonstrations should be banned. On the basis of this antilibertarian fervor, a wide range of more local measures were enacted or advocated during the Gulf War, measures that further illuminate the place of coercion and threat in capitalist democracies. For example, in January 1991, "the district attorney for Suffolk County, which includes Boston, called for bail restrictions on anti-war civil disobedience arrestees to prohibit them from 'participating in this kind of activity in the future' " (Demeter 1991, 3). And "the Boston suburb of Medford—site of Tufts University and anti-war actions," passed "a resolution . . . that encouraged Congress to withdraw federal educational loans and housing subsidies from those arrested 'protesting' " (ibid.). Such calls and resolutions can have effects even when they do not result in enforceable legislation.

It is important to stress, however, that while actions during periods of military conflict provide particularly clear instances of official intimidation (that is, intimidation by some government force or agency), this is by no means confined to such circumstances. Practices ranging from FBI disruption of black organizations (through forged documents, infiltration, etc.; see, for example, Blackstock 1975, chapters 3–5) to the routine police harassment of African Americans walking in upper-class, white neighborhoods would fall under this category. Consider the case of Richard Hill. Driving to a doctor's office in Beverly Hills, he was stopped by two white police officers with their guns drawn and then injured by one of them. Or Patrick Earthy, another black man, "who describes himself as humiliated and terrified by his numerous encounters with the police" in Beverly Hills. He works at a church in the area, and has been stopped and searched eight times in a three-year period—once at gunpoint, another time when handcuffed. The examples could be multiplied (Noble 1996, A14). Their intimidating function hardly requires elaboration.

In addition to legal constraint and official intimidation, there are various forms of popular terrorism that function to the same end. Again, the period of the Gulf War presents numerous illustrations. During the war, there were "arson attacks on mosques in four British towns" and "in northern England, a school bus carrying Yemenis was stoned"; there were also "shootings and attacks on homes" (Lowe 1991). In the United States, "an American-Arab Anti-Discrimination Committee . . . found nearly 100 criminal acts against Arabs . . . including a bomb found in a San Diego mosque and an Arab restaurant burned down in Detroit" (Naureckas 1991,

8). "In Toledo, an Arab-American businessman was beaten by a white supremacist mob. In Kansas City, a gunman fired at a Palestinian family riding in a car. After appearing on a Pennsylvania television program, an Arab-American received seven death threats. . . . Columbia University Professor Edward Said and other Arab-American activists were threatened with assassination" (Kaidy 1991, 18). The list could be extended (see, for example, Novick 1991).

Terroristic intimidation, too, is not confined to wartime situations. Hate crimes against nonwhites have much the same function—sometimes explicitly articulated, as in the case of organized hate groups such as the Ku Klux Klan. Rape and spousal abuse can have a similar function as well. Though they may seem to be purely private or personal matters, they are not. Whatever the motives behind these crimes, they function to intimidate women, to foster conformity, timidity, and so forth. Katha Pollitt (1995) has noted that "fear of rape and attack . . . plays a part in keeping women from claiming public space as their own. We are brought up to be wary."

Antigay terrorism provides a particularly good illustration. Eric Heinze (1995) reports that "in the United States, lesbians and gay men are now considered to be more subject to violent attacks than any other minority group" (7). Twenty percent of gay men and 10 percent of lesbians have been "punched, hit, or kicked"; higher percentages have had things thrown at them, been spat on, and so on (ibid.). But this is far from the worst of it. "Gay-bashing" incidents are often gruesome, sometimes leading to murder and even severe mutilation of the corpse (ibid.). Heinze quotes Richard Mohr, explaining this terrorism: it "has the same social origin and function as lynching of blacks—to keep a whole stigmatized group in line" (7 n. 33).

For such acts of terrorism to have the systematic effect of encouraging conformity, there usually must be some degree of state complicity and/or other structural support (for example, financing from members of a dominant economic group). Such complicity and support are most clear in countries such as El Salvador in the 1970s and 1980s when the terrorist death squads were closely linked with the military, police, and government, sharing much of the same personnel and, ultimately, command structure (see, for instance, Armstrong and Shenk 1982, 77, 86, 101).

This same sort of complicity could be found in the United States during the Gulf War. For example, as Jim Naureckas (1991) pointed out, the mainstream media's "coverage of the 'terrorist threat' sometimes hit the higher frequencies of hysteria," but crimes against Arabs and Arab Americans "were not treated as terrorism" (8). Indeed, these acts of popular terrorism were quite consistent with governmental policies of intimidating harassment and the implicit threat of mass incarceration. More generally, the U.S. government has repeatedly characterized Arabs and Arab Americans as terrorists. Beth Stephens (1991) reported that "the FBI annually conducted an average of 3,000 'international terrorism' investigations during a six-year period in the 1980s. A large percentage of these targeted Arab-Americans. In some, the only basis for the investigation was a connection to a mosque or Arab-American organization." Mainstream media, moreover, came close to condoning acts of anti-Arab terrorism at the time of the war. To cite one case, in an interview with FBI chief William Sessions (16 January 1991), Dan Rather quite rightly expressed concerns over possible terrorist threats against U.S. citizens "of Jewish heritage." He then went on, however, not only to ignore the dozens of real terrorist actions against Arab Americans but also to imply that the rough treatment of Arab Americans may in fact be justified, asking the clearly racist question, "What should our attitude toward Americans of Arab heritage be?" (quoted in Naureckas 1991, 8).

Terrorism was directed at non-Arab peace activists, too. As Don Ogden (1991) wrote, "Prior to a Jan. 15 peace rally, the Springfield Anti-War Coalition was reported to have received a phone call warning that they would be met with baseball bats. Before the Jan. 26 demonstration, the same group was told their busses would be blown up." Threats of violence were not uncommon—as those of us who protested the war are well aware. Moreover, actual attacks were not unknown. These at times received legal sanction, as when a jury in New Mexico decided that certain sorts of comments on the use or abuse of minority soldiers in the Gulf War constitute "fighting words" (see Cohen and Lauria 1991, 8). According to this decision, a peace activist who has used some common arguments against the Gulf War may be physically assaulted and have no legal recourse whatsoever—a straightforward case of structural complicity with terrorism.

There are, again, many peacetime examples of the same sort. Complicity between the Ku Klux Klan and local police forces in the South was notorious. For example, David Chalmers (1981) notes that in the 1920s in Oklahoma, "while the police stood by, men were kidnapped from the streets of even the largest cities. . . . Petit juries refused to convict Klansmen. Victims were afraid to report their whippings to local officials who were often members of the Klan" (52). During the same period, in Arkansas, "Governor Thomas C. McRae was not a Klansman," but he followed a policy of "friendly neutrality" and appointed "a Klansman as his secretary" (57). William Jenkins reports much the same sort of thing in Ohio (see 100–101). Other states could be cited equally.

As for terrorism against gays and lesbians, Heinze (1995) remarks that "such violence routinely goes unpunished or underpunished" (7). He cites one case in which a gay man was beaten to death by a group of teenagers: "The judge imposed no penalty and praised the teenagers' scholastic records" (8, quoting David Greenberg). In another case, a judge gave suspended sentences to a group that had abducted and tortured a gay man; the judge found the perpetrators to be "good boys at heart" (8, quoting Richard Mohr). Moreover, lesbians and gay men in the United States "have been subjected to unprovoked violence by police officers, as well as other forms of police harassment" (8, quoting editors of the *Harvard Law Review*).

The tendency of police to adopt a sort of "noninterference" policy regarding such putatively "personal" or "private" matters as spousal abuse has much the same effect. Again, spousal abuse is an important case of terrorism in this sense. When men physically abuse their wives, this clearly has a consensual function. It not only fosters a subordination of individual wives to their husbands—a crucial part of sex-based hierarchization (or patriarchy)—it facilitates a broader conformity as well. Though its operation is not so obvious as, say, the organized terrorism of the Ku Klux Klan, this sort of private terrorism coerces a wide range of women into conformity with the wishes of men. It batters not only their bodies but their self-esteem, inhibiting their ability to act on their own with a sense of confidence. Like all terrorism, it fosters a general sense of fear that inhibits autonomous action of any type, most obviously including rebellious action. All terrorism encourages fright and passivity, a desire not to change social structures for the better but simply to avoid the brutality of the terrorists—whether these are the Klan or one's own husband.

As just noted, the legal system is broadly complicit with this form of terrorism. This was brought out clearly and poignantly during the O. J. Simpson trial. Simpson repeatedly battered his wife, Nicole, yet Nicole was unable to receive any real police protection. Indeed, the terror induced by spousal violence was painfully evident in the tape of Nicole's appeal to the police for help, recorded when she dialed 911 one evening, having barricaded herself in a room after Simpson attacked her.

Her case is not at all unique. Although statistics on family violence are not precise, the U.S. Department of Justice (n.d.) estimates that "millions . . . are abused physically by family members and their intimates." Susan Faludi (1991) points out that every year over 300,000 battered women can find no emergency shelter (xiv). And spousal abuse is not confined to battery but includes murder as well. Of sex-related homicides, "at least one-third of the women were killed by their husbands or boyfriends, and the majority of that group were murdered just after declaring their independence in the most intimate manner—by filing for divorce and leaving home" (xvii), a point which may have a "deterrent effect" on women who are considering such actions. As to legal complicity, one revealing statistic is that "in thirty states, it is still generally legal for husbands to rape their wives" (xiv).

Harassment is continuous with terrorism. The difference is that harassment neither directly prevents the satisfaction of needs nor threatens one's life or physical well-being. Rather, in the legal definition, it is the creation of a "hostile environment," the cultivation of a sense of alienation and anxiety that inhibits a person's general ability to function. This sort of behavior is illegal, though it obviously continues in many areas. According to the American Psychological Association (n.d.), "Sexual harassment is extremely widespread. It touches the lives of 40 to 60 percent of working women, and similar proportions of female students in colleges and universities" (1). It is far from inconsequential. Sexual harassment can "devastate" one's "psychological health, physical well-being and vocational development" (2).

The obvious cases of this would include insulting or demeaning comments about women, demands for sexual favors, and so forth. But precisely the same effects can be produced by forms of intimidating harassment that are less obviously illegal. For example, it is relatively easy to find some inadequacy in anyone's work. Constant supervision, disproportionate scrutiny of one's performance, harsh criticism for even minor errors all create a "hostile working environment." In addition, they are far more difficult to stop. In situations such as this, the harasser can always claim that he or she simply has "high standards for performance." The victim often has no way of responding to the harassment, other than complaining that no one else is subjected to similar scrutiny. But, of course, the harasser can always rely on the circular response that other workers have not been found to require such supervision, as they are more competent. This sort of thing is found all the time in the treatment of women and nonwhites in academia, as when nonwhites' publication records are subjected to a thorough criticism, with every possible flaw investigated, while whites' publication records are hardly given a second thought.

Workplace hostility is not the only way in which intimidating harassment might occur. Consider, for example, the general distrust and scrutiny of blacks in our society. Philomena Essed (1991) notes that "shop personnel pretend they are going about their usual business, but . . . Black customers are put under strict surveillance" (224). I myself experienced a striking case of this when I was in a bookstore with a nonwhite friend. It was an afternoon, and we were the only two people in the store. We were both looking through books in a leisurely manner, but at one point, she was told that she should buy the book she was looking at or leave. My browsing gave rise to no such imperative. This, too, has an intimidating and thus consensual function, for it gives members of the dominated group the sense that they are under constant observation and threat of censure.

INFORMAL COERCION: SOCIAL DISDAIN
AND FEAR OF NONCONFORMITY

The diffuse danger of critical scrutiny from one's immediate society is less intense than threats from the police or the fear of terrorism, yet in many ways it is more pervasive. Indeed, perhaps the most routine or habitual form of coercion is not a matter of overt violence, or any punitive action, but rather the largely silent disapproval and withdrawal of one's peers. Aristotle (1984) contended that humans are social animals, so much so that "no one would choose to possess all good things on condition of being alone" (1169b). As such, the broad denial of respect, love, and basic sociability, and its replacement by snubs, hard stares, or general indifference, is almost as painful to us as battery. Reinhold Zippelius (1986) has argued that such denial is continuous with current criminal law, aspects of which appear to have developed out of systematic social "shunning," ostracism, and related practices. Its effectiveness is unsurprising. As Carol Barner-Barry (1986) explains, "Exclusion from the group is painful in that it deprives an individual of the protective and nurturant functions of the group, thus exposing that individual to a greater risk of physical or psychological damage" (291).

This social pressure is never a pressure to excel. It is never a pressure to change the social structure—even if such a change would benefit the group in question. Rather, it is always a pressure to conform, to proceed in the normal way, to do what everyone else is doing. John Stuart Mill (1971) described the phenomenon well when he noted that, typically, individuals do not ask themselves, "What do I prefer?" or "What would allow the best and highest in me to have fair play, and enable it to grow and thrive?" Rather, they ask, "What is usually done by persons of my station and pecuniary circumstances?" (309). People "exercise choice only among things commonly done" (310). This is not because of some depravity of spirit. It is, instead, because social opinion has the same sort of consensual force as law. Although less intense, it is almost certainly more constant. As Mill put it, aptly drawing on the parallel with a legal system, in society at large "peculiarity of taste, eccentricity of conduct, are shunned equally with crimes" (310).

The most obvious element of this pressure to conform concerns matters that are generally considered moral—sexual practices, for example. Mill rightly maintained that "to extend the bounds of what may be called moral police, until it encroaches on the most unquestionably legitimate liberty of the individual, is one of the most universal of all human propensities" (332). Compulsory heterosexuality provides a clear instance, particularly appropriate here because it indicates the range of social pressures that bear on conformism. Many gays and lesbians have an entirely legitimate fear of publicly revealing their sexual preference, even in states where discrimination based on sexual preference is officially illegal. Suppose a gay man is living in an area where homosexuality is not criminalized. Nonetheless, he decides to marry and lead a "respectable" life. Why would he do this? Ex hypothesi, it is not a matter of possible legal repercussions. There is, of course, the constant threat of terrorism. That is real and significant. But perhaps more important is the broad range of disabilities that go along with social disapproval. The most extreme case of this is the loss of employment. Even in states that outlaw discrimination based on sexual orientation, it is a simple matter to find reasons for ending someone's employment, and easier still to find reasons for not hiring someone in the first place. Such antidiscrimination laws are valuable on several fronts. First of all, they impede discrimination by forcing employers to make a case against the gay or lesbian person in question. Perhaps more crucially, they establish a sort of counternorm to the broad homophobia of society, and thus, create an alternative to that sort of conformity. Nonetheless, they hardly prevent discrimination.

Beyond this, even if one feels secure in one's employment, declaring oneself gay has a wide range of consequences in relation to social disapproval—consequences often slight in themselves, but cumulatively very hurtful. For example, gay men sometimes find people squeamish about touching them, even shaking hands, evidently for fear of some sort of contamination. Witness the bizarre incident at the White House where secret service agents wore rubber gloves to greet a delegation of gay elected officials (White House 1995, A26; and Rich 1995, 15). Or they may find themselves excluded from social events—not necessarily out of animosity but out of a sort of awkwardness about inviting "normal" male/female couples and one gay couple. The list could be extended, but the point should be clear.

Of course, the pressure to conform is hardly confined to moral issues. Even in the case of homosexuality, the primary impetus behind social disapproval seems to be more visceral than ethical—a matter of the disapprover's own repressed homosexual impulses, as a recent study has indicated ("individuals who score in the homophobic range and admit negative affect toward homosexuality demonstrate significant sexual arousal to male homosexual erotic stimuli" [Adams, Wright, and Lohr 1996, 443]). The social disabilities just mentioned can affect any persons whose nonconformist actions—sexual, political, or whatever—could be considered controversial. Any sort of unusual behavior, including visibly nonconformist political behavior, can be deleterious to one's career. Individuals engaging in such behavior can find themselves uninvited to social events and so on. I am not referring only to militant revolutionism. The point holds for simple, local acts of ordinary humanity insofar as these break with common practices, and thus operate to challenge those practices. I know from my own experience that the merest suggestion that a tenure committee is treating a nonwhite candidate prejudicially will produce broad social disdain verging on ostracism—all the more so if the suggestion is well-founded. In other words, suppose a tenure committee is indeed subjecting a nonwhite candidate to unusual scrutiny and criticism. Any mention of this fact—including the most mild, unofficial suggestion—will be met by an almost universal insistence that the tenure committee has been subjected to a Stalinist attack of unspeakable cruelty and that the perpetrator of this heinous crime should be duly punished, by official censure, if possible, or at least by ostracism.

The threat of social disapproval can extend to many more trivial matters as well. One's coworkers may be highly judgmental about whether one buys a house; what part of the city one lives in; whether one goes to church, and where; what books one teaches in a particular course (Are there "too many" women on the list? Is it "too noncanonical"? etc.); where one eats lunch; and so on.

Here, one might reasonably wonder what gives rise to this particular form of coercion. Jones conforms because, otherwise, he or she will be excluded from the comforts of human society. But why are Jones's colleagues and neighbors so insistent on conformity? There are two obvious reasons. The first is that nonconformism implies a sort of threat to the social habits of other members of the group. This is true in an obvious way if the nonconformist behavior directly challenges the morality or rationality of the conformist behavior. For example, if someone indicates that a group is treating minorities in a discriminatory manner, that is a direct challenge to the moral legitimacy of the general group behavior. But even in other cases, this is a potential risk. If Jones teaches many noncanonical authors in a literature course, this is not necessarily a moral challenge to his or her colleagues (perhaps the noncanonical authors are white men). But Jones's act nonetheless establishes a competing paradigm for the course in question. It sets up an alternative that students or future faculty may find preferable.

One could think of the problem this way. Each of us develops what might be called a "practical identity." This is one's internalized set of habits, routines, expectations, and so forth. It is what allows one to move through daily activities with ease, to coordinate one's actions unreflectively with the actions of others. This involves everything from such explicitly formalized matters as driving (where we can drive, what signals to make and look for, how to interpret signs, etc.) to such implicit matters as what sorts of sentiments one can express with friends (for instance, when it is appropriate to sign a letter "Love," "Affectionately," or whatever), what sorts of vocabulary one can use in what contexts (classrooms, dinner parties, professional meetings), and so on. Almost the entirety of our daily lives is built up on this set of unreflective expectations and practices, for which some degree of broad social conformity is clearly necessary. Individual nonconformism is almost invariably perceived as a threat to that practical identity.

Indeed, it very often is a threat. Homosexuality, antiracism, even innovation in teaching can make aspects of one's practical identity problematic or unworkable. Such nonconformism may even indicate that aspects of that identity are deeply inconsistent with one's own moral ideals or self-interests—and hence, that one's daily life and the broader structures in which it unfolds have been seriously misguided, dishonest, or simply unnecessary, pointless. In A *Proper Marriage*, Doris Lessing (1964) illustrates this powerfully in the person of Mrs. Knowell, an older woman who opposes the rebellious, antipatriarchal actions of Martha Quest—in particular, Martha's impending abandonment of her husband, Douglas: "Mrs. Knowell lay awake night after night . . . crying steadily. . . . [S]he felt betrayed by Martha. Her own life was made to look null and meaningless because Martha would not submit to what women always had submitted to" (336).

The second reason for social hostility toward nonconformism is simpler. Standard behavior is not salient; it is just the opposite with unusual behavior. What is odd gets noticed, and what is common goes unremarked. If everyone is in a suit, but one person is in a jogging outfit, the jogging outfit seems strange. If everyone is in a jogging outfit, but one person is in a suit, the suit is what stands out. This has two consequences. First of all, in drawing attentional focus, salience draws scrutiny. It is rather obvious that one's flaws are much more likely to be noticed if one is scrutinized than if one "blends in" and is not scrutinized. In part, the social disapproval aimed at nonconformists is simply a matter of recognizing flaws (or apparent flaws) in the nonconformist because he or she has been subjected to particular scrutiny.

One sees this sort of thing regularly in academic evaluations, from tenure cases to book reviews. The novel idea is subjected to a rigorous critique, whereas the accepted idea passes by unquestioned. (There is extensive research indicating this; see Hogan 1993, including the citations.) In a notorious case at the University of Connecticut, a tenure candidate was working in an almost entirely new area and with almost entirely new theories (relative to other members of his department—in fact, the field and approach were well established in the profession as a whole). He also lived in a different area from his colleagues, had rather different interests, etc. He had a book forthcoming from a major university press, which is ordinarily enough to assure tenure without question. This particular case, however, was scrutinized more strongly, at least in part because the candidate and his work did not "fit in." Once the scrutiny began, evaluators asked a number of unusual questions, ones that simply did not arise in parallel cases—for example, how much the book overlapped with the candidate's dissertation. As a consequence, they ordered a copy of the dissertation for comparison. I understand that the book differed significantly from the dissertation, but the important point does not concern the relation between the dissertation and book. Again, that was not a standard question; it was not an issue that arose for candidates who fit in. Rather, the extra scrutiny to which this person was subjected when being considered for tenure and the results of that extra scrutiny are key here.

In addition to scrutiny, saliency tends to draw affect. In a fairly obvious way, people are more likely to feel strongly about someone who is an object of attentional focus than about someone who blends in. This feeling is not invariably negative, yet in the ordinary course of things, negative feelings tend to outweigh positive ones in terms of their practical consequences. For example, one person's vehement opposition to hiring a particular (unusual) job candidate is likely to overshadow someone else's enthusiasm for that candidate—at least if there are less controversial candidates. In any context of threat, moreover, the feelings are far more likely to be negative than positive. Finally, the affect associated with attentional focus often involves a psychoneurotic component (specifically, a "transference" [see chapter 3]) that is volatile and can shift easily from positive to negative—which is perhaps even worse than a consistently hostile attitude.

ECONOMIC CONTINGENCY
Perhaps the most common reason people conform is not the threat of violence, terror, or ostracism but in Marx's famous phrase, "the dull compulsion of economic relations" (737). The need for food, housing, and clothing requires us daily to reproduce the relations of production, for they not only stifle but sustain us. First of all, most of us have neither time nor energy to rebel. As Friedrich Schiller put it, in a statement that ap-

plies as much today as it did two centuries ago, "The greater part of humanity is too much harassed and fatigued by the struggle with want to rally itself for a new and sterner struggle" (49). Our lives are stiff with necessary routine, insensible with tense insecurity and isolation, hedged by crowding tasks. Juliet Schor (1991) has shown that the average person in the U.S. labor force works the equivalent of fifty-four forty-hour work weeks in a (fifty-two-week) year (29). In keeping with this, Robert Frank (1999) notes that in "a recent Gallup Poll, 39 percent of respondents reported working more than 45 hours a week, one in eight more than 60" (50). Employed mothers, Schor estimates, average about sixty-five hours of work per week, in and out of the home. She emphasizes that "overwork is . . . rampant among the nation's poorly paid workers" (21). As a result, Schor adds, "A third of the population says that they are rushed to do the things they have to do" and "half the population now says they have too little time for their families" (11). In connection with this, most people in the United States sleep "between 60 and 90 minutes less a night than they should" (11). This is not only a symptom of overwork but a cause of further problems as "chronic sleep deprivation contributes to many serious illnesses" (Frank 1999, 51). In addition, "stress-related diseases have exploded" and are most severe among those in low-level assembly line jobs (Schor 1991, 11).

Indeed, on the whole, the less privileged members of society have the worst health and worst health care. For example, in a U.S. Bureau of the Census study from 1984, there was (unsurprisingly) an inverse correlation between income and time without health insurance; people in the bottom quintile were more than five times as likely to lack medical insurance as people in the top quintile. More important, less than 2 percent of those in the top 40 percent of income reported having poor health; in contrast, over 20 percent of those in the lowest 10 percent reported having poor health (see U.S. Bureau of the Census 1992, 39; see also U.S. Bureau of the Census 1991, 165, 168). A decade and a half later, the situation is the same or worse. According to a 1998 study from the Center for Disease Control, "Low income adult men were seven times as likely to be uninsured as high-income men and low income women eight times as likely as their high-income counterparts to be uninsured." Moreover, "For almost all health indicators considered, each increase" in income "increased the likelihood of being in good health. This relationship between socioeconomic status and health was observed for every race and ethnic group examined" (Socioeconomic Status 1998; on health insurance, see also Guyer and Mann 1999).

These conditions make it quite difficult to begin or sustain any sort of resistance. Consider the simple economics of a strike. In the late nineteenth century, Peter Kropotkin explained the repeated failure of worker revolt by noting that "the 'average working' person existing from one pay-packet to the next, had 'no reserve funds upon which to live.'" In consequence, "within a few weeks of 'economic disturbance,' hunger and want became a mighty force that inevitably led to compromise with capital and state. Within a very short time the workers . . . will be 'compelled to submit to any conditions'" (quoted in Purchase 1996, 158). One might imagine that this situation is different now than when Kropotkin was writing, and in some ways it is. But the crucial limitation of workers' resources remains the same. Indeed, the problem is hardly confined to laborers. It is part of a broader economic insecurity. As Robert Frank (1999) observes, "Half of respondents in one national survey reported life savings of less than $3,000." Forty percent would find it difficult to deal with an unexpected expense of $1,000 (96). It is not only blue-collar workers who are "existing from one pay-packet to the next" and thus have reason to fear any disruption in ordinary economic processes.

Even if people do have the energy, health, time, and short-term resources needed to rebel, they risk sacrificing the long-term benefits they currently have, however limited. If this point needs to be documented, some striking cases are reported by Susan Faludi (1991) in Backlash: "At N BC, two female producers who had played key roles in a sex discrimination suit against the network were forced out and replaced by inexperienced young white men— at the same salary. At the New York Times, all the named plaintiffs in [a] sex discrimination suit suffered major career setbacks, and most had to leave the paper" (375). The situation is, of course, the same in the blue-collar world. A particularly horrifying instance is that of American Cyanamid, which forbade women from working in a higher-paying department unless they were surgically sterilized. Several employees brought suit. OSHA ruled against the company. But, as Faludi reports, "The women who participated in the suit would be among the first laid off in the '80s. And when they went looking for work elsewhere, they found that their reputations as troublemakers had preceded them" (449). As a result of such practices, which became more widespread in the 1980s, Faludi asserts that "women became increasingly reluctant to fight discrimination collectively" (375). Much the same could be said for other groups. The Program of the Labor Party (n.d.), "A Call for Economic Justice," states that "today, nearly 1 out of 10 workers involved in union organizing drives is illegally fired" (5). Sometimes the punishment is not individual but collective. For example, Annette Fuentes (1997) notes that "more than 50 percent of employers threatened to stop operations" when there was a drive to unionize workers. Worse still, "when unions won their elections," "companies shut their doors" at "three times" the average rate (6). In other words, when a group of workers simply decides to unionize, they triple the likelihood that their company will close, leaving them unemployed.

To a great extent, the conditions that make U.S. society undesirable—overwork, excessive stress, economic insecurity—are the same ones that render rebellion dangerous, and therefore unlikely. Consider, for example, job insecurity and the problem of unemployment. The mere fact of unemployment is a constant threat to and source of stress for workers, for it is a reminder that one might lose one's job at any time. A 1995 survey found that 46 percent of workers were "frequently worried about being laid off" (Frank 1999, 52). This is true not only because the unemployment of others stands as a sort of testimony to the fact that employment is insecure; more important, unemployed and underemployed workers provide a "surplus labor pool," as many writers have remarked. Should any individual worker prove difficult, there will always be another worker, nearly desperate from unemployment and anxious to take the first worker's place. This implicit threat not only inhibits worker activism; it also operates to reduce wages, benefits, and more, and for the same reason. The larger the pool of surplus labor, the less leverage workers have in any conflict with owners over wages, benefits, safety, or whatever.

Part of the purpose of the recent welfare "reform" is directly in keeping with this. The release of a large number of people from welfare operates to benefit business and harm workers. This is especially clear when one recalls that this alleged reform was initially handled through the institution of subminimum wage jobs and the exclusion of "workfare" participants from labor rights, such as unionization and standard labor laws (see, for example, Workfare Rights 1997, 10). Unsurprisingly, a study by the Center on Budget and Policy Priorities (n.d.) showed that as a result of welfare reform, "poor families became poorer." The "weakening of safety net programs" led to this "increase in the depth of poverty for the average poor family." The intimidating consequences for the labor force as a whole hardly require elaboration.

Another recent development that exacerbates insecurity is the widespread increase in positions that are neither permanent nor full-time. College and university teachers are familiar with the loss of tenure-track positions and the dramatic rise in part-time instructorships over the past decade or so. It is in the nature of such instructorships that they lack security extending beyond a single semester or, at best, nine-month academic year. This situation promotes conformism in obvious ways. While a permanent employee must not be so offensive as to provoke dismissal, a temporary employee must be so inoffensive that he or she will actually be rehired after the term his or her contract expires.

Higher education is not by any means unique in this reduction of permanent employees. Molly Ivins (1999) cites a recent AFL-CIO study showing that "thirty percent of workers are in contingent jobs—part-time, temporary, on-call or contract work." Moreover, "Forty percent of the young employees say it is all they can get."

IMPOSED DEPENDENCY AND MYSTIFICATION
The final sort of negative self-interest I would like to isolate is perhaps not properly referred to as a form of coercion at all. It is not so much a fear of any particular outcome, as a sort of generalized fear or paralysis of will arising from dependency. Put in the simplest terms, people often do not pursue even their own most elementary rights, at least in part, because they do not have the knowledge or skills to do so, but are dependent, or feel so, on particular people or a particular job.

Until quite recently, this was most obviously a problem for middle-class women. Even when abused by her husband, a woman might well hesitate to leave him, especially if she had little education and experience in the labor force, and had been a wife and mother for many years. Such a woman would hardly even know where to begin if she wished to seek economic independence. Fortunately, this is much less true than it was, say, thirty years ago.

In some ways more important than such confusion and uncertainty about employment is confusion and uncertainty about the legal system. As already noted, the law is frightening enough on its own, threatening enough, coercive enough. But it is all the more intimidating insofar as it is incomprehensible. An abused spouse may be less constrained by ignorance of the job market than by ignorance of the law—uncertainty as to even how to proceed with legal action. The same holds true for a wide range of workers as well.

This is a pervasive and serious problem. The law is involved with all aspects of coercion: not only with police matters but with intimidation, as well as aspects of terrorism. Moreover, it is crucial to the operation of economic insecurity—for procedures of dismissal and hiring, negotiation over wages, health benefits, and so forth, are at least in part governed by law. Ignorance of the law prevents people from using those aspects of the law that do in fact aid the miserable. The law is, after all, a sort of patchwork, made up over many years by people from different backgrounds, in different circumstances, with different interests. Its broad structure clearly operates to preserve economic stratification. Despite this, there are many specific elements of law that genuinely protect human rights outside of or even in opposition to that stratification.

Not understanding the law has the effect of fostering a sort of hyperconformism. When uncertain about what sort of behavior can or will be punished, many people will behave in the most cautious way possible. Put simply, when one is faced with an entity that is threatening, and unpredictable, one is likely to do everything in one's power to just stay out of its way.

Finally, while law is a particularly important case, this is true more generally. Ignorance of the principles governing intimidation or terrorism—their nature, origin, and function—makes these forms of coercion all the more threatening and effective. Like ignorance of the law, ignorance of the political economy of coercion tends to foster hyper-conformism, a severe conservatism or overcaution induced by a deep, but vague fear of powerful forces that one does not understand.

This is what marxists have traditionally called "mystification." And it is a crucial, coercive (or perhaps "metacoercive") element in fostering consent as well. The point is not unknown in empirical social science. Lee Ross and Richard Nisbett (1991) ask, "How does one respond when 'nothing seems to make sense,' when one's own understanding of the actions and outcomes unfolding around one obviously is limited or deficient?" Basing their analysis on experimental studies, they suggest that "few people . . .

would respond by acting decisively or asserting independence. Rather, they would become uncharacteristically indecisive, unwilling and unable to challenge authority or disavow role expectations, and highly dependent on those who calmly and confidently issue orders" (58).

NEED, DESIRE, AND DEMAND

But again, rational or "calculated" acquiescence is not solely a matter of coercion or negative self-interest. It involves positive elements, too. Any given society systemically defines a set of possible desires and achievements for its members or classes of its members. Thus, in an advanced capitalist economy, certain things are possible for working-class people, such as the acquisition of material objects (televisions, VCRs, etc.). Other things are not possible, such as economic security. One's short-term interests necessarily urge one to pursue the possibilities inherent in the current system, not those outside the system.

In order to discuss the nature of these interests and possibilities, some terminological distinctions should be drawn. The influential French psychoanalyst Jacques Lacan distinguished three types of human goals: "need," "desire," and "demand." I will be borrowing these terms from Lacan, though I will be assigning them somewhat different meanings. By "needs," I mean goods, services, living conditions, and so on, the absence of which has a systematically and continuously deleterious effect on the physical or emotional health of people thus deprived. Simple cases of needs in this sense would include, say, vitamin C—the absence of which systematically degrades the health of the body. But needs here also include a variety of nonconflictual social interrelations, a basic sense of respect from one's immediate community, an engagement in productive work, and so forth—for the absence of these systematically degrades one's emotional health. Put differently, one does not "adapt" or "get used" to need deprivation; nonsatisfaction of a need continues to have deleterious effects on one's health.

By "desires" or "objects of desire," I mean goods, services, conditions, and the like, the acquisition of which will, one imagines, bring one pleasure (or relief from unpleasure), but which have no necessary, particular role in emotional or physical health. "True desires" refers to those desires aimed at objects that will in fact produce pleasure; "false desires" are those aimed at objects that will not produce pleasure.

By "demands," I mean simply anything one sets out to acquire or achieve, independent of whether one genuinely needs or desires it. Note that demands may be aimed at objects of need, true objects of desire, false objects of desire—or objects for which one does not feel any particular motivational impulse. There are objects of need and desire that one demands, objects of need and desire that one does not demand, and objects of demand that one does not need or desire (even falsely).

Though largely universal themselves, being based on human biology and psychology, needs and true desires are not satisfied in an abstract, universally identical manner. Rather, they are organized into a structure of demands and constraints on the satisfaction of demands. This is true both absolutely and relatively. Consider physical needs. "Absolutely," within any given society, only certain sorts of housing, food, or clothing are available. The society produces these and not others. Every society has its technologies and physical conditions that determine what can and cannot be done, as well as rules and practices that determine what is allowed and disallowed (for instance, laws that constrain building, or that regulate the growing and selling of agricultural products). "Relatively," not all forms of housing, and so on, are equally available within a given society. Most obviously, they are differentially accessible according to one's economic status. Hence, some people can afford any available housing; others can afford only the least expensive, least satisfactory housing; others cannot afford any housing whatsoever.

This is also true of nonphysical needs and desires. Clearly, the need for productive work can be pursued only within the options available to individuals in any society—those available to the society as a whole, and those available to members of society in one's own particular social position. Similarly, the human need for companionship is channeled into particular means of meeting others and particular modes of socializing with them. For example, in U.S. society, one interacts with a potential spouse in very specific ways—through particular sorts of activities, with particular conventions.

There are, again, universal elements to all of this. But the cultural particulars are most crucial for understanding social consent. Specifically, this socially definite channeling of need serves, among other things, to identify needs with their particular modes of pursuit and satisfaction in society—the "system-internal" modes of pursuit and satisfaction, as might be said.

In this way, such channeling serves to foster consent. The need for a thorough relationship with another human life, a relationship that allows one to feel and communicate security and affection, is plainly a much more general need than its instantiation in, say, middle-class American marriage. The need to pursue such a relationship is clearly open to far more various expressions and developments than U.S. dating practices. The need for productive labor is not confined to the options available within the economic system in the United States. But in each case, the more abstract need is regularly identified with its concrete manifestation in this specific society.

The important consequence of this is that one comes implicitly to identify one's need not as a need for a particular sort of relationship but as a need for marriage as it is understood and structured in this society; not as a need for rewarding and productive labor but as a need for a particular sort of job in the current social organization. (Here and below, precisely the same principles apply to desire; they, too, are socially specified and tacitly reduced to such specifications, with the same consensual consequences.)

This does not mean that people are satisfied with the current situation. Within a highly stratified society, few people are likely to feel that their needs are genuinely met. The identification of needs with system-internal options for fulfilling those needs, however, serves to channel that dissatisfaction to system-internal alternatives or ideals as well. So, dissatisfaction with one's marriage is not directed at problems with the structure of marriage in U.S. society. Rather, it is particularized, seen as a problem with the specific marriage—not insofar as it *does* conform to the pattern of marriage practices in the United States but as it does *not* conform to that pattern. My point is not, of course, that marriage problems are never particular or a matter of deviation from an American ideal; it is that all those problems that arise from the structure and operation of American marriage—which may account for the majority of marriage difficulties in the United States today—are precisely the problems that are, most often, ignored.

Consider, for example, the stereotypical husband whose wife has stayed home raising the children for the past decade. He grows dissatisfied as he begins to feel that they no longer have anything in common. He views her as dull in comparison with his female colleagues at work. But when she returns to work, he continues to be dissatisfied, now because she is no longer home to take care of all the housework, cooking, and so on. He finds that she wants him to take on some of the work at home, even though he already feels overburdened from his own job. (Obviously, she has the same feeling; his resentment may be understandable, but it is not justifiable.) If his dissatisfaction becomes acute enough, he may decide that this particular marriage is wrong, that he would be better off with a different spouse. But it seems much more likely that the problem is with the structure of American marriage itself—or rather, the structure of American marriage as it is located in the larger network of structures in American society.

The same is true of work. Sometimes one's sense of alienation at work is the result of a particular job. Often, though, it is the result of the structure of and options for work in U.S. society. Insofar as needs tend to be identified with actual social options for satisfying those needs, people fail to recognize that dissatisfaction may result from the limited nature of those options. Insofar as problems with marriage or work in the United States are conceived of as solvable by pursuing a better (American) marriage or job, people do not consider that the problem may stem from the inadequate social structure available for human interaction or productive labor. Insofar as individuals think and act along these lines, focusing entirely on system-internal options, the pursuit of their own needs will keep them firmly within the bounds of social consent, despite the fact that the pursuit of personal needs should be the greatest force driving individuals to break those bounds of consent.

Beyond this, demands are often steered away from work or love, even within their systemic limits. To a great extent, in an advanced capitalist society such as the United States, different physical and emotional needs and desires are reduced to consumption. As a number of writers have noted, the United States "may be the most consumer-oriented society in history" (Schor 1991, 107), driven by a frenzied cycle of "earn and spend" (128)—or more accurately, "spend and earn," for consumer culture is one of long-term, structured indebtedness (see Calder 1999). Demand is continually structured as demand for commodities. Chris Rasmussen (1999) argues that for consumers faced with "an abundance of products," "pleasure-seeking is channeled in directions that reinforce . . . the capitalist economy" in obvious ways (20).

What is more, it seems that this demand for commodities frequently has no basis whatsoever in need or desire, even false desire. It often appears to be *mere* or what might be called "hollow" demand—in some cases, a matter of quantitative accumulation only, a demand for "things," "lots of goods . . . more goods this year than last year" (Calder 1999, 7). In keeping with this, psychological research indicates that "across-the-board increases in our stocks of material goods," such as have occurred in the last fifty years, "produce virtually no measurable gains in our psychological or physical well-being" (Frank 1999, 6). Given the hollowness of these demands, what draws people into consumerism—not once only but repeatedly?

Juliet Schor (1991) explains the ordinary person's acquiescence in the spend and earn cycle as the "result of habit formation and relative status considerations" (128). This seems true, if only partially so. Specifically, tendencies toward imitative conformity, most obviously developed in response to social coercion and threat, are exacerbated by the particular conditions in which need and desire are experienced. Finding themselves dissatisfied, and unable to think of needs outside the structures imposed on those needs by the current social situation, people are likely to view their dissatisfaction as a sort of fearful mystery. They feel unhappy, but don't know why. Here as elsewhere, this uncomprehended dissatisfaction is most likely to promote extreme caution in the exercise of autonomous judgment. Though confusion and fear may well be consequences of prior conformity, individuals generally react to these feelings by conforming still further. In part, this is because, already feeling vulnerable, people cannot bear the thought of being the object of collective scrutiny, and thus, perhaps the object of collective hurt. But it is also because, uncertain as to why they are unhappy to begin with, confused as to the causes of their dissatisfaction, individuals are likely to turn to other people in order to see what they want, on the assumption that what other people want must be what would make those individuals themselves happy as well. This is not, most often, a conscious process of inference, but a more immediate, imitative response. It is, in a sense, a response to a type of mild panic. Individuals may have no genuine desire, even a false one, for a particular sort of car, television, or home. Yet they may pursue these due to a sort of spontaneous imitation of their neighbors, or families on television, who have these things and appear to be happier.

Putting the point another way, it might be said that the inability to imagine system-external goods is part of a broader inability to imagine the restructuring of society. What the Greeks called *eudaimonia*, "the good life," is unavailable, not only in practice but, effectively, in conception as well. One might say that the social system does not provide the material basis on which to imagine eudaimonia concretely outside the options set out within this society. This not only inhibits dissent. By depriving humans of broader social goals, this social system fosters a sort of active conformism—in, for example, imitative consumption, as just mentioned.

On the other hand, not all evidently frivolous consumption falls into this category. At any given level of economic achievement, in fact, seemingly irrational consumption may be a genuine, if contingent, *system-internal* need. Specifically, beyond channeling and organizing universal human needs, societies create objects, activities, services, and the like that allow individuals to function within that system. For instance, when I accepted my present job, the only accommodations I could afford were inaccessible by public transportation. I had virtually no choice but to own a car. It became a contingent or system-internal need. In this way, systemic imperatives force people to pursue goals that have little or no intrinsic value for them, but are crucial for their intrasystemic success or even survival. Such needs are systemically created. Moreover, they are systemically created needs that perpetuate the system against people's larger—extrasystemic—interests.

Finally, once someone has organized his or her life around achieving those goals that a society allows—getting a promotion, owning a house, etc.—and has actually met some of those goals, he or she not only becomes a supporter of the system through unreflective practice but also has reason to desire the continuation of the system more positively and self-consciously (as noted above in connection with hostility toward nonconformism). In any functioning society, not only what is desired but almost everything individuals have actually achieved, have worked toward achieving, or are about to achieve, is defined by the system that is in place. As Friedrich Schiller wrote (1954), "On the very deceptions which the hostile light of knowledge should dissipate, they have based the whole structure of their happiness, and are they to purchase so dearly a truth which begins by depriving them of everything they value?" (49–50). Indeed, people may resist this truth all the more strongly to the degree that it confirms the sense of nagging dissatisfaction they have felt all along, but have been unable to recognize and articulate, and make the basis for action.

A further aspect of self-interest strongly conducive to conformity may be found in the elaboration of the economic structure in which one's achievements and acquisitions are located. Every society hierarchizes its members in such a way as to grant each stratum some degree of relative privilege with respect to system-internal goals. Put simply, in any society, virtually everyone is better off than someone else. Advanced capitalist societies such as the United States rely extensively on this microhierarchization. While the distribution of wealth in this country is grossly imbalanced, those who have had steady employment for some time are better off than those now in entry-level positions, those who have temporary employment are better off than those who are unemployed, those on welfare are better off than those whose benefits have run out, and so on.

This has several consequences. To begin with, in the context of an ideology proclaiming universal social mobility, it offers the prospect of incremental advancement "up the ladder of success." In this way, microhierarchization fosters commitment to the system as a whole, for it offers a prospect of success within the system. The precise nature of this potential success, moreover, is coordinated with the structure of system-internal demands. It is what permits the sorts of satisfaction allowed by the system, such as consumer goods. More important, at every level of success or failure, people realize not only what they might gain but what they might lose; they realize that the system has allowed them something that they could be denied, that they have achieved some systemic goal that they might not have achieved, that they suffer less economic insecurity than they might.

Note that both the positive and negative factors of microhierarchization oppose one's interests to those of one's coworkers. This sort of structure turns everyone into competitors for advancement and threats to one another's security. Microhierarchization encourages, for example, entry-level workers to see one another not as allies against management but as competitors within an insecure system—a tendency often actively fostered by employers.

Perhaps the most common function of microhierarchization is to fragment working people along lines of race and gender, for any type of fragmentation and hierarchization is more effective insofar as it can attach itself to salient, noncontextual properties, such as race or sex. As such, it is related to the more general process of "interest differentiation": the cultivation of distinct and contradictory interest groups within an oppressed class. For instance, Todd Gitlin (1995) notes that "many companies" go so far as to "encourage the growth of particularist organizations in the workplace." He cites "the anti-union Digital Equipment Corporation," which "cultivates groups of women, blacks, and gays" (226) in a strategy that clearly operates to undermine encompassing worker organizations. Insofar as women at the company are encouraged to see their interests as gender based, blacks are encouraged to view theirs as race based, and so on, workers' collective sense of class-based interests is likely to be weakened, even when this differentiation is not strictly a matter of microhierarchization.

Of course, interest differentiation operates most effectively—and most pervasively within this economic system—when it does involve microhierarchization. As Etienne Balibar and Immanuel Wallerstein (1991) have stressed, capitalist economy requires flexibility in employment practices. In times of expansion, capitalists need more labor; in periods of contraction, they need less. But it is difficult for employers to hire and fire at will with no repercussions. They risk the rise of a united working class, demanding continuous employment. One solution is to microhierarchize the working class by race and sex, so that members of a dominated group (blacks, women) take up the lowest-level positions in times of economic expansion, but then return to unemployment when the economy contracts. As Wallerstein explains, racism "allows one to expand or contract the numbers available in any particular space-time zone for the lowest paid, least rewarding economic roles, according to current needs" (34). This does not have to be a matter of self-conscious design by employers. The structure might develop in various ways—most obviously as the result of prior racist hierarchization (for example, in the period of slavery, which was certainly self-conscious). But having developed, it "works," and thus, tends to be stable and independent of any person's self-conscious intention.

To say that this microhierarchization works is simply to say that insofar as blacks are being laid off, white workers are less likely to see themselves as threatened, and therefore, less likely to offer resistance to employers. Indeed, the benefits to whites over blacks are obvious, and strongly discourage unity between these two groups. Edward Wolff (1996) points out that the median white family has twenty times the wealth of the median nonwhite family (2). This discrepancy will only increase as long as the median income of blacks is just slightly above half that of non-Hispanic whites (U.S. Bureau of the Census 1998, vii). As for women and men, Susan Faludi (1991) contends that "nearly 75 percent of full-time working women [are] making less than $20,000 a year, nearly double the male rate"; "the average working woman's salary still lag[s] as far behind the average man's as it did twenty years ago"; and "the average female college graduate today earn[s] less than a man with no more than a high school diploma (just as she did in the '50s)" (xiii; the situation has improved some since Faludi's research, but the general point still holds [see U.S. Bureau of the Census 1998, 34–37]). In these and related cases, microhierarchization clearly functions to discourage broad solidarity and concerted opposition of the deprived majority against the wealthy minority. In short, it fosters consent.

Though race and sex appear to be the most widely significant and enduring instances of this sort, microhierarchization—with the resultant class fragmentation and conflict—may operate through religious, ethnic, and other divisions as well. Moreover, microhierarchization and class fragmentation are by no means confined to industry. Class fragmentation is, in effect, a form of the divide-and-rule strategy that was employed self-consciously by colonial governments—as illustrated by the British colonial policy of setting Hindus against Muslims in colonial India (see, for example, Sarkar 1973, 14–18, 80), or more recently, by the practice of separating and opposing Zulu, Xhosa, Tswana, and Sotho in apartheid South Africa (see Lapping 1989, 180; for other instances of the same type elsewhere in Africa, see also Rodney 1972, 79–80).

Microhierarchization fragments in other ways, too, as when an employer opposes the interests of different employment groups that would not otherwise be set in conflict with one another ("In the next budget, we have to cut either the secretarial or janitorial staff"), or when fine distinctions within a group are formalized. For example, I was struck recently by the fact that in my department, one of our clerical workers is termed an administrative assistant, one is called a secretary, and two are labeled temporary support staff. Department administrators insist to the administrative assistant that she is more like an administrator than a secretary—

though her salary is, of course, not even close to being in the same range and she has no administrative power; and the administrative assistant also emphatically insists that she is not a secretary. All such strategies of microhierarchization function to divide, tying the systemic successes of individuals to that division. Systemically, it is a success to be a secretary, not temporary support staff, or an administrative assistant, not a secretary.

This leads to the final function of microhierarchization, or rather, the final way in which it operates to fragment groups that should be working in solidarity. Distinctions of title or salary grade are not merely a matter of short-term self-interest. They are also a matter of self-esteem. Unfortunately, it appears that few people's self-esteem rests on the accomplishment of goals or the satisfaction of standards that they have set for themselves. Indeed, it seems that few people's self-esteem is founded on aspiration and accomplishment at all. Rather, to a great extent, people's self-esteem appears to rely on their feeling that they are in a dominant position over someone else, or that some group to which they belong and with which they identify is in a dominant position over another such group. Many studies have shown that given a choice, most people would rather maximize their superiority over others than gain more for everyone, including themselves. As John H. Duckitt (1992) summarizes, "Group members . . . seek maximum relative advantage for the ingroup over the outgroup, even when this interferes with the achievement of maximum absolute outcomes for the subjects" (85). In keeping with this, suppose subjects "are categorized into minimal groups," that is, divided arbitrarily into groups distinguished by name only (such as "A" and "B"). If members of one group "are given the opportunity to discriminate [against members of other groups], they . . . show increased self-esteem" (ibid.). More generally, T. A. Willis (1981) has suggested that "downward comparison"—contrasting oneself with those lower in some hierarchy—is extremely important to one's self-image, and that people "can increase their subjective well-being through comparison with a less fortunate other" (245).

This disturbing psychological factor clearly operates to make hierarchies all the more powerfully functional in undermining solidarity, and serves to attach everyone more strongly to the system of stratification. Except for those at the very bottom, it adds yet another system-internal satisfaction, and hence, another motivating force for consent.

Beyond the "primary" interests discussed so far, in certain cases, disprivilege may carry "secondary gains" as well. People learn to adapt to the conditions in which they find themselves. Then they come to rely on the gratifications those conditions present, however meager. Anyone is unjustly deprived if he or she is denied the right to pursue a career—whether through sexism, racism, or poverty. But having been denied that right, one may come to appreciate not having responsibility for one's condition or future, and all that results from that responsibility or is associated with it (for example, the significantly decreased life expectancy for men, which is roughly 10 percent below that for women [see USA 1998, 48; and Jolly 1999, 138]). Secondary gains are seductive and foster consent. It is hardly surprising that when someone has been denied his or her basic rights, he or she often clings to secondary gains.

More exactly, there are two sorts of benefits that fall under the category of secondary gain. The first is purely negative. It is the benefit of not having to struggle for success thereby risking failure. The second benefit is positive and involves an attachment to any genuine advantages of the oppressed position. Negative secondary gain is common to virtually all oppressed groups. Typically, members of such groups are disallowed certain possible achievements and, at the same time, are told that they would fail if opportunities were available. Thus, for example, women have historically been denied access to careers in mathematics and have been told that they are incapable of doing such work. In these circumstances, some women come to accept their position and rely on not having to prove themselves in difficult mathematics courses—a particularly important reliance as many of them believe that, as women, they cannot do mathematics. It is thus unsurprising that many women acquiesce in an educational division that disprivileges them. The point is generalizable. Referring to business, Cynthia Epstein (1988) has argued that "women . . . are lured by secondary gains . . . which remove them from the risks as well as the rewards of competition in the world of affairs in which men labor" (234).

It is worth noting that negative gain is not merely a sort of pitiable surrender but has quite robust emotional appeal. It is not *experienced* as negative. Psychological research indicates that lack of success, even outright failure, when "attributed to external causes," such as "prejudice and discrimination," "protects self-esteem" and "leads to no more negative affect than does success" (Crocker and Major 1994, 292). In other words, being able to attribute one's failure to racial prejudice, sexism, or any other nonmeritocratic factor protects one's feelings of self-worth in the same way that actual *success* does—success that would hardly be guaranteed if the system were, in fact, meritocratic.

Positive secondary gain is more limited, yet still widespread. It consists of the benefits one experiences in one's condition as subordinate. Courtship practices, for instance, give women some slight financial gains, which can be significant depending on the context. In high school and college, the amount of money spent on a date can be a substantial burden to the man, and can make a real difference to a woman who might not easily be able to afford a dinner out or a movie. Not being sent into combat is another obvious, positive secondary gain. Clearly, these are slight in comparison with the losses. Dating practices come nowhere near compensating for women's loss in income due to discrepancies in hiring, promotion, salary, and the like. Women's exclusion from combat, while crucial for those women who might otherwise be killed in battle, does not concern the vast majority of women, and hardly compensates for their general exclusion from the governance structure of the country, including that of the armed forces. Such gains, however, are real, palpable, salient. Equality is a mere dream, impalpable, a promise. Thus, positive secondary gains too foster consent, foster a commitment to the current order of things.

Margaret Atwood (1985) illustrates this well in *The Handmaid's Tale*, where Offred begins to take pleasure in certain aspects of her generally horrid existence and then finds that she no longer wishes to escape (348). She does not want to lose what little she has for the uncertain possibility of something better, even far better. "Truly amazing, what people can get used to, as long as there are a few compensations," she observes (349).

ETHICAL IMPULSE, THE JUST WORLD,
AND MORAL MYSTIFICATION

There is one sort of impulse that has been passed over in the discussion of need, desire, and demand: the impulse toward virtue. It provides a nice transition to a look at ideology. I do not share the view—held, it seems, by the majority of men and women—that moral convictions have deep consequences for one's behavior. One continually hears politicians stressing the need to instill moral feeling in the youth of this country so that they do not join gangs, sell illegal drugs, engage in street crime, and so forth. But it seems clear that these activities have relatively little to do with internalized morality. Rather, they are largely the result of social conditions, even the narrow circumstances of daily life. As numerous psychological studies have shown, there is a tendency to assume that people's actions are based on deep convictions and personality traits. Yet for the most part, they are a mere result of environmental contingency.

Consider, for example, a well-known study by J. Darley and C. D. Batson (for a summary and discussion, see Holland et al. 1987, 226–27). This study sought to determine what factors entered into one's personal decision to help or not help someone in physical distress. The researchers began by determining the degree to which the test subjects felt a personal, ethical commitment to works of mercy. They then contrived to put their subjects in a situation in which they would have to decide whether or not to help a suffering person. Specifically, the subjects were sent out from the building. Half of them were told that they must hurry to another building because they were expected there and were already late. The other half were told that they should proceed to the other building, but that there was no great hurry. On leaving the first building, the test subject was faced with an injured person needing help. The researchers discovered that an ethical commitment to works of mercy did not predict whether the test subjects helped the injured person. Instead, the best predictor of whether a test subject would assist an injured person was whether or not the subject was in a hurry.

Studies such as this indicate that the impulse to virtue has, in fact, relatively little bearing on people's actual behavior in the world. Notwithstanding, most people probably do have a deep emotional need to think of themselves as behaving ethically. It is important, in other words, for emotional health that individuals not conceive of themselves as bad or evil but as fundamentally good. That is consequential, even if one's (stated) ethical beliefs are not. Furthermore, it is consequential in a way directly relevant to the fostering of social consent.

Every society of which I am aware involves contradictions between precepts and practices. This is obvious in predominantly Christian countries, such as the United States, where Jesus' injunction to divest oneself of riches has been perverted into an imperative for the accumulation of wealth, where the central precept of nonviolence has been twisted into

jingoistic militarism, and so on. More generally, people in any economically stratified society are perfectly capable of looking around and recognizing that some people are or appear to be suffering due to no fault of
their own, while others are or appear to be enjoying ill-gotten gains. If this
is true, if indeed the miserable many do not deserve their misery and the
opulent few do not merit their wealth and power, then one's own conformity with the system is a form of complicity; one's imitation of the standard modes of behavior is an aping of immoral practices.

How, then, does one respond to this dilemma? One option would be to
change one's behavior, to act according to the moral precepts, not the
common practices, thereby setting oneself at odds with one's society. This
is, of course, overwhelmingly unlikely, given the great motivational force
pushing against such a change and the almost insignificant part played by
ethical commitment in people's actual practical lives. In addition, if anyone
really does pursue such a course, he or she is swiftly punished. The mass of
society reserves particular scorn for anyone who tries to act according to
moral principle. Indeed, they take special care to denounce him or her as
morally reprehensible. For anyone who spurns social convention in order to
abide by society's moral precepts is, as such, a forceful argument that the
rest of society is not behaving morally, that its affirmation of principle is
mere hypocrisy. Action according to moral principle is the most threatening form of nonconformism. The only way of undermining the effect of
such a person's example, the disturbing implications of his or her action, is
to brand him or her a hypocrite and reprobate. This was the attitude of the
Athenians to Socrates or the Pharisees to Jesus.

So, what is the alternative? It is simple: assume that the world is in fact
just. Once one makes this assumption, it is easy enough to work out the
details, should one wish to do so (which is also unlikely). One simply
considers each seeming contradiction until one finds how the apparent
opposites are reconcilable. After all, they must be reconcilable, for it is a
just world ex hypothesi. Though Luke's account of the Beatitudes praises
"the poor" and "the hungry" (6:20, 21), for example, Matthew refers, more
comfortingly, to "the poor in spirit" and "those who hunger . . . for what is
right" (5:3, 6). Matthew allows one to reconcile the admonition to abandon one's riches with the daily accumulation of wealth—for one can convince oneself that one has indeed abandoned one's riches *in spirit*.

It might seem that this sort of thinking is rather limited, and if not limited, then at least innocuous. But it is neither. Research in cognitive and social psychology indicates that this "just world" thinking may be a "universal tendency." As John H. Duckitt (1992) explains, the work of M. J. Lerner and his colleagues suggests that "individuals have a basic need to believe that they live in a world that is a just . . . place where people generally get what they deserve and 'deserve what they get' " (153). As to being innocuous, just world belief leads directly to consensual conformism, and even to sometimes vicious forms of victim blaming. "Becoming aware of an innocent victim threatens the belief in a just world and motivates strategies to protect this belief. . . . An important strategy used is that of derogating the victim and seeing the suffering as deserved." In keeping with this, one may attribute "negative characteristics to [victims] to explain their misfortunes" (ibid.). Indeed, the belief in a just world tends to become stronger to the extent that one is faced with blatant injustice. One researcher "compared just-world beliefs in matched white South African and British samples. The belief in a 'just world' was significantly higher in the South African sample," which is to say, among those living every day in the system of apartheid (ibid.).

Voltaire's parody of Gottfried Wilhelm Leibniz in *Candide* is brought home by a continual reiteration of the following theme: "It must be for the best, for this is best of all possible worlds," grotesquely chanted, with variations, after every horror, from natural disasters to mass killing. "Here old men, stunned from beatings, watched the last agonies of their butchered wives, who still clutched their infants to their bleeding breasts; there, disemboweled girls, who had first satisfied the natural needs of various heroes, breathed their last; others, half-scorched in the flames, begged for their death stroke. Scattered brains and severed limbs littered the ground. . . . [A]ll events are . . . arranged for the best . . . everything is for the best in this world" (137, 138–39). This appears ludicrous, an absurd exaggeration, but it is in fact not far different from most people's ordinary mode of ethical thinking. As Voltaire indicated, this belief permits people to live comfortable lives amid misery, comfortably performing the most unjust acts in conformity with the status quo. Indeed, by fostering victim blaming, it may exacerbate the injustice of these acts.

It is worth noting here that it is not only oppressors and third parties who commit themselves to believing that the world is just. The oppressed do so as well. Often, the victims also rely on a belief that the world is just, for it helps them to survive their victimage. In *The Handmaid's Tale*, Margaret Atwood (1985) tells how Janine accepts the cruelty of the society that oppresses her, accepts the idea that her suffering is deserved ("She thinks it's her fault"), because she wants to believe that what she is doing makes sense, has a point, is right: "People will do anything rather than admit that their lives have no meaning" (279). The consensual effect in this case is too obvious to require explanation.

A form of character evaluation closely related to just world thinking is interesting in this context. Research indicates that people share a tendency to infer properties of individuals from their social roles (see, for example, Hamilton and Trolier 1986, 156–58). As David Hamilton and Tina Trolier comment, "It seems plausible that the content of American racial stereotypes may be at least partially a function of the differential social roles predominantly occupied by whites and blacks in this society" (158). Perry Curtis (1968) points to the same phenomenon among some Victorian English and Scots for whom "the relative paucity among Irishmen of skilled workers and professional men proved beyond all doubt that the Irish were an inferior people incapable of self-help and therefore unfit to govern themselves" (15). The researches of A. H. Eagly and V. J. Steffen, discussed by Hamilton and Trolier, provide considerable support for the view that this is the case for stereotypes about men and women. This cognitive tendency is strongly consensual, for it in effect infers the appropriateness—and by implication, justice—of the status quo from the mere existence of the status quo. For example, before the recent influx of women into medicine, it would have led people to infer from the predominance of female nurses and male doctors that women have nursing talents and men have doctoring talents, and as such, the most fair and reasonable system made men doctors and women nurses.

One final aspect of ethical feeling is worth considering here. Perhaps there are some times when ethical choice may, at least in part, guide one's thought and behavior. For instance, ethical choice might play a role when one undertakes some action that is unobserved, and thus, less immediately prone to conformism—such as voting on a tenure case. If so, it is clearly crucial that people be able to reason out the ethical alternatives. Typically, ethical choices in real life are complex. Indeed, they would hardly face individuals as choices if they were not. Whether to buy a gun and shoot some innocent person just to release frustration—this is not a moral "hard case." Whether or not to award tenure to a particular candidate may be more difficult.

Again, I do not wish to exaggerate the importance of moral principle in such decisions. It is, in fact, rarely key, and probably never decisive. But if it is ever to enter at all—as in, per the above, a tenure decision—people must be able to engage in moral reasoning. Spontaneous moral impulses are an incoherent flux of empathy and self-interest, overgeneralization and excessive specification. Careful moral reasoning is, in the first place, a way of determining what one thinks, what one believes morally. Moral reasoning involves determining what general principles one holds, what their implications are, how they relate to concrete situations, which of these principles might be relevant to the case at hand. It involves testing generalizations to determine whether they are excessive, ill formulated, or based on concealed self-interest. This all seems straightforward. Still, most people make wild mistakes about their own ethical beliefs. It takes considerable work to determine not what is right or wrong in and of itself but simply what one believes to be right or wrong. As "Aristotle stresses (and as Socrates showed before him), most people, when asked to generalize, make claims that are false to the complexity and the content of their actual beliefs. They need to learn what they really think" (Nussbaum 1986, 10).

When discussing ethical issues in undergraduate classes, to cite one case, my students regularly claim that if someone believes a certain act to be morally right, then it is morally right. But no one who makes this claim actually believes it. Indeed, it is easy to show students that they do not believe this. For example, a Nazi thinks it is morally right to kill Jews. But no one in the class really believes that this makes killing Jews morally right, even for a Nazi. Timothy McVeigh thought that blowing up government buildings was morally right. But no one in the class really believes that this makes blowing up government buildings morally right, even for McVeigh. My students do believe that conscience has a role in determining moral choice. Yet they greatly oversimplify their belief when they try to express it as a generalization. As a result, they will often come to conclusions about particular ethical cases—hard cases—that are inconsistent with their own implicit, complex views.

This confusion and vacillation about one's ethical beliefs is only exacerbated by the sophistic forms of ethical inference put forth by political and religious figures in justification of what should appear as uncontroversially unethical practices (for instance, the mass murder of civilians in war). All of this serves to mystify ethics and so push ethical decision also in the direction of imitative conformity, for people tend to resolve their ethical confusions by reference to standard views and behaviors much as they resolve their uncertainty over needs and desires by reference to standard demands. Thus, the limitations of people's untrained moral reasoning tend to render their ethical decisions consensual in those few cases where they might otherwise have had independent force and thereby worked against consent.

TWO   *Belief and Consent*

Positive and negative self-interest are clearly powerful factors in fostering consent. Nonetheless, at any given time, it is likely that there will be a number of people who are seriously disaffected with the current structure—most obviously the bottom 20 percent who have almost nothing to lose by change. Given that the middle 60 percent are receiving less than their equitable share, it is likely that their consent will be unstable as well, at least insofar as it arises from rational or calculated self-interest alone. In other words, self-interest may not be adequate to prevent the most miserable from developing significant antipathy toward the current structure, even to the extent of engaging in active resistance. And it is unlikely to foster a deep commitment to the status quo on the part of those in the "middle," who form the majority of the population and could potentially be radicalized by the actions of the most deprived. It is at this point, of course, that more overt coercion enters. Yet systems that rely too heavily on coercive force are inefficient. They are wasteful of resources, breed popular discontent, and are frequently unstable for that reason. As Laura Anker, Peter Seybold, and Michael Schwartz (1987) argue, "Violence and other means of repression (e.g., court cases, public denunciation, and executive orders) may prove counterproductive, dampening the enthusiasm of, or even alienating, those who would otherwise support" a particular social structure (99). This is where "internal coercion" or "ideology" becomes significant—guiding behavior through shaping ideas, producing consent by structuring thought and feeling.

The most obvious component of ideology is belief. Indeed, in concrete political analyses, consensual ideology is often treated almost entirely in terms of belief. The first function of ideology, after all, is to foster in people the sense that the current system is right, that it is beneficial, that alternatives are threatening, and so on. In short, it operates to overcome the consensual deficiencies of positive self-interest, without recourse to coercion. This is first of all a matter of belief—if belief that is more intricate, varied, and complex than may at first be obvious.

BELIEFS, SYSTEMS OF BELIEF, PROBLEMATICS, AND FOCALIZATION

Whether people acquiesce or not in a certain social structure is, in large part, dependent on what they believe about that social structure, about themselves, and about the possibility of alternative structures. To a great extent, dominant ideology (ideology that fosters consent to the status quo) is a matter of beliefs that conceal oppression—from the oppressors, the oppressed, and those who fall into neither or both categories—and deny the possibility of an alternative, nonoppressive society.

In addition, consent is crucially dependent not only on what specific views are held to be true but also what views are considered to be possible, what claims might be considered as even potentially true. An ideology that fosters consent, in other words, operates both by encouraging positive beliefs and setting the terms of debate so as to exclude certain sets of possible beliefs from consideration or discussion. The latter is called "establishing the problematic," the problematic being the range of beliefs that are open to evaluation, debate, and the like.

The Gulf War abounds in examples of both consensual beliefs and problematics. Anyone who had occasion to discuss the war with its enthusiasts came to realize that their support was most often based on extensive erroneous beliefs. A February 1991 study by the Center for Studies in Communication at the University of Massachusetts at Amherst showed that there was "a direct correlation between knowledge and opposition to the war" (Jhally, Lewis, and Morgan 1991, 51); false beliefs systematically correlated with support for the war (that is, systematically produced consent). As the authors noted, "Supporters of the war . . . were more than twice as likely to wrongly assert that Kuwait was a democracy than non-supporters" (ibid.); "While support for the war appear[ed] to be strong, it [was] built upon a body of knowledge that [was] either incorrect or incomplete" (52).

As to the role of the mainstream media in producing error and thereby manufacturing consent, the researchers found a strong positive correlation between viewing television news and holding erroneous beliefs: "Overall, the more TV people watched, the less they knew. The only fact that did not fit in with this pattern was the ability to identify the Patriot missile" (50).

It is important to emphasize that these mistaken beliefs are not isolated but part of *systems of beliefs* that are mutually sustaining and "confirming." For example, common ideas about the Gulf War fit into a system of beliefs concerning U.S. foreign policy in general, past U.S. wars, and so forth.

The Amherst survey gives a striking case of this. Not taking into account the postwar results of the U.S. bombardment, "the figure for Vietnamese casualties [in the Vietnam War] is just under 2 million." Nonetheless, "the median estimate of Vietnamese casualties by respondents in our survey was around 100 thousand, a figure nearly 20 times too small. This is a little like estimating the number of victims of the Nazi holocaust at 300 thousand rather than 6 million" (52). Mistaken beliefs of this sort contribute to the plausibility of a whole series of further beliefs, from the general notion of the humaneness of U.S. war practices to the specific idea that the allies were killing almost no one in the Gulf War bombardments. These and other related beliefs work together, supporting one another in a system, each belief or complex of beliefs rendering all the others more plausible.

A particularly interesting misconception about the Vietnam War concerned the peace movement and Vietnam veterans. It was, of course, the U.S. government that sent troops to Vietnam, exposed them to death or permanent harm from enemy fire as well as U.S. defoliants, and refused to grant them certain medical and other benefits when they returned. It was the peace movement—many members of which were Vietnam veterans— that tried to bring the troops back and thus remove them from danger, that set up counseling and other services for veterans, that worked for Agent Orange related medical benefits, and so on (see, for instance, Lembcke 1991). Nevertheless, it was widely believed during the Gulf War that the peace movement of the 1960s was responsible for the suffering of Vietnam veterans. Thus, it came to be widely believed that protesting the Gulf War was contrary to the interests of the U.S. troops—a view that approaches psychotic delusion, but that was widely held and so quite powerful in effecting consent precisely because it fit into this broader system of belief.

The same points apply equally to racism or sexism. The effects of false beliefs—such as that women cannot do math, or that blacks are not as intelligent as whites—have obvious consequences that hardly require articulation. They lead, say, to the exclusion of women from mathematics courses (by parental decision, the advice of counselors, the decision of women themselves); they lead to the denigration and undervaluing of blacks.

Problematics are in some ways more subtly pernicious—even when the dominant belief in the problematic is ideologically innocuous. Dan Rather's question, "What should our attitude toward Americans of Arab heritage be?" implicitly includes within the range of possible or debatable opinions the racist idea that Arabs may be treated differently from other Americans and that guilt may be presumed in their case. Although this view came to be rejected in the course of the interview, it was clearly part of the larger debate that this question tacitly sanctioned. Rather's question—in the context of the broader discussion of terrorism—also implicitly excludes from the range of possible opinions the idea that Arab Americans are prime victims of terrorism. In this case, the specific belief affirmed in the course of the discussion—that Arab Americans are not necessarily terrorists—is less important than the problematic defined by the entire interview.

Problematics not only structure and limit general debate on socially consequential issues; they also guide individual thought and inference, even for those who appear to have rejected the relevant biases. Consider, for example, the problematic defining race and intelligence. One accepted position is that blacks are intellectually inferior to whites, and that this is biologically determined. Another is that blacks are inferior, but that it is socially determined. A third is that blacks and whites are equal in intelligence. Suppose Professor Smith, who is white, has decided that blacks and whites are equal in intelligence. He or she has still made that decision within the context of the broadly accepted problematic. Smith has a black, British student named Jones. Smith discovers that Jones responds in an unclear way to readings and class lectures. In addition, Smith finds it hard to understand Jones. Again, Smith does not believe that blacks are in general inferior to whites intellectually. In the context of the socially accepted problematic, however, Smith is likely to interpret this particular case in terms of Jones's intellectual capacities. In contrast, had Jones been white, Smith might have assumed that it was a matter of, say, regional accent, idiom, and vocabulary. Smith might even have entertained the possibility that the problem was a special intelligence or conceptual complexity on Jones's part. In cases such as this, elements of the consensual problematic provide the set of options within which particular problems are thought through—even when one does not accept those elements self-consciously.

In any discussion of ideology, it is essential to distinguish self-conscious beliefs from what might be called "motivational" ones. Self-conscious beliefs are those that people take themselves to hold on particular issues, that they state when asked, that they admit to themselves. Motivational beliefs are those that actually guide thought and action. Such motivational beliefs may be identical with self-conscious beliefs. Indeed, in the vast majority of cases, they necessarily are. Yet they are different in a surprising number of cases—especially cases of social and political importance. For example, while I may be entirely subjectively certain that I believe women and men are equally intelligent, I may repeatedly treat women as if they were incapable of grasping difficult concepts; I might talk in a patronizing manner, overexplain simple ideas, etc. Here, it is clear that my motivational belief is the opposite of my self-conscious one. My behavior reveals that my motivational belief is that women are less intelligent than men. The case of Smith, just mentioned, is slightly more complex, but follows the same pattern. Specifically, it might be said that Smith's self-conscious belief is compromised by a motivational problematic.

Still broader issues are encompassed by ideological problematics as well. Consider the way in which alternatives to the present social system are conceived. In ordinary parlance, "capitalism" and "democracy" are used as virtual equivalents, and "communism" is treated as a subcategory of "totalitarianism." Totalitarian communism is fairly consistently presented as the single alternative to "capitalist democracy," directly or indirectly. The propaganda surrounding the Vietnam War was largely a direct representation of this view, for instance. Once this problematic is established, it becomes difficult even to bring such alternatives as "democratic socialism" into the discussion. Not only are such alternatives left out of official debate; they appear to be largely incomprehensible to the majority of ordinary men and women as well.

More exactly, the standard version of the problematic defining social structure divides social ideals into two broad categories, realistic and utopian, with U.S. capitalism and Soviet communism as the two realistic poles. Note that this sort of problematic inhibits one's ability to conceive of alternatives to the present system in realistic terms. By reducing realistic alternatives to the single case of the Soviet Union, it renders opposition to the current system undesirable. Complementary to this, it undermines the motivational force of truly worthwhile social alternatives by characterizing them as imaginary and unworkable.

The point can be clarified by drawing a distinction between "utopias" and "visions," the latter being Noam Chomsky's (1995, 70) term for genuinely desirable and possible alternatives to the present society. The purpose of a social vision, in this sense, is to serve as a measure for evaluating the current system and a guide for changing that system. A utopia—in the sense of an unreachable and purely imaginary ideal—can serve neither function. Being unreachable, it cannot guide action; being an impossible ideal, a mere fantasy, it cannot reasonably be employed to evaluate the current system. By characterizing as utopian all alternatives other than the USSR, the dominant problematic regarding social structure effectively excludes any possibility of social vision.

This problematic itself is part of a more general narrowing of the idea of eudaimonia or human flourishing. Consider the operation of religion in this regard. In a famous phrase, Marx referred to it as "the opium of the people" (244). The analogy indicates that religion is a form of distracting pleasure that numbs people to their own oppression. But, perhaps even more important, religion operates to co-opt the vision of eudaimonia, and it does so in the service of the present system. Much as a commercial society fashions people's material demands from the impulses of their legitimate needs, religion (or at least officially dominant religion) forms nonmaterial desires out of people's legitimate aspirations toward eudaimonia. Whether it urges people to seek heaven or nirvana, it turns their sights away from establishing a real eudaimonic society here and now; it encourages them to aim for an ideal life beyond this world or in detachment from it. Indeed, it often does this by fostering social consent in specific and overt ways. To take only one of many possible examples, the role of Christianity in the colonial domination of Africa was, as Walter Rodney (1972) has noted, "primarily to preserve the social relations of colonialism, as an extension of the role it played in preserving the social relations of capitalism in Europe." In order to achieve this end, "the Christian church stressed humility, docility, and acceptance," and "preach[ed] turning the other cheek in the face of exploitation" so that "everything would be right in the next world" (252–53). Finally, and in some ways most crucial, consent-inducing religion distorts people's conception of a eudaimonic society, for it encourages them to conceive of eudaimonia as a mystical, posthumous, individual communion with divinity, as an emotive withdrawal from material life, and the like, rather than as a practical community of men and women freely working together in thought and action to achieve justice, prosperity, and beauty in all their lives.

Not all religion is consent inducing, of course. Historically, there are cases of religious movements that push against the status quo. The ideological function of religion, however, is most often consensual. After all, the religious views that receive the support of the powerful in a society— and thus, typically become the dominant ones—will invariably be views that support the position of the powerful. To take one example of this, the connection between social hierarchy and religious belief is particularly well established in regard to racism. C. Daniel Batson and Christopher Burris (1994) point out that there is a "positive correlation between being religious and being [racially] prejudiced" (165), such that "church members tend to be more prejudiced than nonmembers, irrespective of the target of prejudice" (Duckitt 1992, 174–75).

A further aspect of consensual ideology closely related to the establishment of problematics is focalization. Focalization is merely the focusing of attention and discussion on one topic or aspect of a situation. Take, for instance, the British conquest of the Igbo. A primary component of their ideological justification for this concerned the Igbo practice of human sacrifice. But the English defeated the Igbo by mowing them down with automatic weapons, killing far more people than would have been sacrificed had the English never encountered the Igbo. As Elizabeth Isichei (1976) put it, "The wars fought to establish colonial rule in Igboland" were "fought in the name of the abolition of human sacrifice, but no historian will ever be able to count the number of human sacrifices they exacted" (139). The Igbo practice was certainly objectionable. Those who believe it is wrong to kill innocent people certainly agree that the practice should have been stopped. At the same time, those who believe it is wrong to kill innocent people should also agree that the British slaughter of thousands of Igbo was far more wrong, if only because the murder was far more extensive. On this particular issue, the British did not so much rely on false beliefs (the Igbo did indeed practice human sacrifice) or the establishment of a problematic. Rather, they focused attention on one aspect of the situation, to the exclusion of all others. (Of course, they also relied on beliefs and problematics about other aspects of the conquest of Igboland.)

A less obviously bloody example—but one involving deep human suffering nonetheless—may be found in the recent debates over welfare, which focused almost entirely on the apparently staggering costs of the program and on adult recipients. Yet Aid to Families with Dependent Children (AFDC) "cost taxpayers approximately $14 billion per year during 1995 and 1996—only 1 percent of the federal budget" (Defund Corporate Welfare 1997). Two-thirds of the recipients of AFDC are children. All recipients need the money—in the basic sense of the word "need." Corporate welfare, in contrast, fell completely outside the debate, though it "totals more than $167 billion per year" (ibid.)—a dozen times the cost of AFDC. Needless to say, this money does not go to poor children. The focus on AFDC expenditures served to occlude the far more extensive, and incomparably less justifiable, corporate welfare, among other things.

As the preceding examples already indicate, ideologically functional focalization is most often bound up with ideologically functional beliefs, systems of beliefs, and problematics. The debate over affirmative action is one such case. Clearly, this has operated to establish a problematic on minorities, hiring, and education—the limits of debate being confined roughly to whether or not affirmative action has gone too far in advancing minorities. (In fact, affirmative action does not seem to have come at all close to compensating for racism, but this view is excluded from debate a priori.) At the same time, this debate has served to focus attention on minority hirings and admissions to schools. As such, it has tended to focus white people's blame for problems associated with work or education (for example, unemployment) on those minority hirings and admissions, often with serious practical consequences.

Consider the famous case *Regents of the University of California v. Bakke* (438 U.S. 265, 98 S. Ct. 2733, 56 L.Ed.2d 750 [1978]). Bakke had applied for admission to the Medical School at the University of California at Davis. He was denied admission, despite such qualifications as high test scores and grades. His claim in the suit was that his rejection was an instance of reverse discrimination because 16 of 100 places in the class were set aside for minorities. Bakke did indeed have better scores than the average student awarded one of these 16 reserved places. But he also had better scores than the average student admitted by the regular admissions procedures. This fact, however, went undiscussed. The entire debate around the case centered on the minority spots, ignoring the places occupied by the many white students whose scores were inferior to Bakke's. Put differently, Bakke's suit maintained that Bakke should have been admitted over the minority admittees due to his credentials. It entirely left aside the fact that his qualifications put him above a much larger number of white admittees. Specifically, in 1974, Bakke's academic qualifications "were superior to at least 42 *regular* admittees, but he sued the university on the grounds that his qualifications were superior to those of 16 *minority* admittees" (Hogan 1998, 234). Though it may not be obvious at first, this exclusive attention to the minority slots is quite similar to the British focus on human sacrifice among the Igbo.

Problems with the Bakke case are, no doubt, not only a matter of focalization. Clearly, the biased interpretation of the data—or ignoring of the data in favor of a prior conclusion—was bound up with racism as well, if not on Bakke's part, then on the part of the larger society that was much more likely to give credence to a complaint of reverse discrimination than to one of censorship. (Bakke's rejection seems to have partly resulted from political disagreements with the chair of the admissions committee, and in that sense, seems to have involved genuine free speech issues.) On the other hand, focalization is crucial to this case and many like it.

Indeed, even the narrow attention to "qualifications" is itself partially an ideological focalization. Do higher grades and SAT scores necessarily indicate that someone is a superior candidate for medical school? First of all, there is the issue of the degree to which grades and SAT scores might be biased. It seems immediately clear that there is at least some bias in the verbal component of these tests—given differences between black and white forms of English. But that is hardly the whole of it. There is considerable evidence that even in such supposedly "pure" cases of logical inference as mathematics, people do not rely on rules of logic but on "pragmatic reasoning schemas" drawn from their own experience (see, for example, Holland et al. 1987, 277–79). Odd as it may seem, individuals are better able to solve problems if they concern familiar topics than unfamiliar ones, even though the topic is irrelevant to the logic of the problem. If I bake, but do not row, then I will be better able to solve a mathematical problem about baking than rowing. This is another likely source of bias in such tests, given that different racial groups often have systematically different types of experience in this country.

Second, and perhaps more important, the purpose of training doctors is, one assumes, to advance the medical care of the entire population. Insofar as black doctors are more likely to treat black patients, and less likely to do so in a racist way, there is a social need for increasing the number of black doctors. Penda Hair (1996) observes that "highly respected studies show that minority physicians are much more likely to treat poor and minority patients whose medical needs are not being met by the existing crop of doctors" (12; Hair goes on to note that "the same public benefit probably also flows from diversity in law schools and other fields of study"). Tom Hayden and Connie Rice (1995) actually followed up the Bakke case in this regard. They report that Bakke "ended up with a part-time anesthesiology practice in Rochester, Minnesota." They contrast him with "Dr. Patrick Chavis, the African-American who allegedly 'took Bakke's place' in medical school" and who now "has a huge OB/GYN practice providing primary care to poor women in predominantly minority Compton." They ask, "Bakke's scores were higher, but who made the most of his medical school education? From whom did California taxpayers benefit more?" (266). The focalization on merit, defined unreflectively in terms of grades and test scores, leaves such issues as these out of consideration as well.

MEANS OF ESTABLISHING CONSENSUAL IDEOLOGY

Before turning to some further categories of belief that have a special ideological function, it is worth considering for a moment just how ideological beliefs, systems of beliefs, problematics, and focalizations are defined and disseminated.

The primary way in which ideologically functional beliefs are disseminated is pretty obvious: through false statements that foster consent and the concomitant suppression of true statements that are damaging to the dominant system of ideas. The most blatant case of this is censorship, one intersection of ideology with coercion. This may appear to have no relevance in the United States, yet that is untrue. For example, it is well known that U.S. newsmedia in Saudi Arabia were subject to rigorous censorship during the Gulf War (see, for instance, Full-Court Press 1991). According to an article in *Extra!* (Spin Control 1991), "Reporters who tried to cover the war outside the Pentagon's press pools were sometimes detained and threatened by U.S. soldiers. Marines held a wire service photographer for six hours, threatening to shoot him if he left his car—'We have orders from above to make this pool system work,' they told him. A French TV crew was forced at gunpoint to turn over to Marines footage of soldiers wounded at the battle of Khafji." Moreover, censorship was not always governmental. "When Jon Alpert, a stringer for NBC news for 12 years, came back from Iraq with spectacular videotape of Basra and other areas of Iraq devastated by U.S. bombing, NBC president Michael Gartner not only ordered that the footage not be aired, but forbade Alpert from working for the network in the future" (Casualties at Home 1991, 15).

Wars, of course, are unusual and intrinsically newsworthy events. If one's country is at war, it is almost certain to be a major topic of reporting. Thus, something along the lines of censorship is required if unsavory facts threaten the official picture. The situation is somewhat different with respect to events or conditions that might be considered less obviously newsworthy. In these cases, the "wrong" sorts of story are usually not pursued from the outset, though when they are, censorship may result. For example, "the dangers of fiberglass—currently in 90 percent of American homes—as a possible cause of lung cancer" is one of those conditions that is not likely to be a focus of media attention. It happened that ABC's *20/20* did undertake an investigation. The network, however, "bowed to the $2 billion-a-year fiberglass industry and yanked the story" (Douglas 1996, 17).

But again, most stories of this sort do not require censorship, as they simply never arise. John McManus (1994) notes that "organizational culture normally steers reporters away from sensitive topics before a confrontation point by defining response to certain public information needs as beyond the resources the firm is willing to commit to news, or outside the proper purview of news" (26). Indeed, much of the exclusion is even more mechanical than this implies. There are vast areas of socially consequential events and conditions that are removed from coverage structurally, by the organization of the media—where reporters are sent, how papers or broadcasts are organized, and so on. Once the structure is established, it tends to be self-perpetuating.

Consider local television news. Susan Douglas (1997b) points out that according to one study (which looked at Detroit), "only 2 percent of the local news focused on the government and politics—that translates into eighteen seconds! There was zero coverage of poverty, education, race relations, environmental problems, science, or international affairs during the two months of the study." She adds that "watching the local news . . . you would never know there was a state legislature, a state court system, or a governor"; in contrast, over 50 percent "of nightly news stories [are] devoted to crime and disasters" (ibid.) This is of particular import at the present time because of the devolution of responsibility for public programs, such as welfare, to state government. Again, it does not appear to be a matter of overt censorship but rather a function of the organization of the news itself—the structure of topics, the placing of reporters, etc.

Discussing local television news, McManus (1994) remarks that "most commercial stations purchase research on how to select, gather, and report news profitably from a relatively small number of news consulting firms," all of which give similar advice. One result of this is the establishment of common procedures, and hence common exclusions, across stations. More exactly, McManus divides local television news production into three stages: "uncovering potentially newsworthy issues and events"; "choosing among those events and issues"; and "reporting the story" (88–89). The bulk of news "discovery" (stage 1) is "passive." Television stations find their stories in "local and regional newspapers or wire services or in press releases," in part because this is much less expensive than hiring a lot of reporters (96), and the reporters they do hire are overworked. At one station, "no reporter said he or she could spend more than a few minutes a day looking for newsworthy events" (100). As such, one-quarter of the stories at this station "were submitted by public relations agents" (100). Others came from routine "morning phone calls to police and fire dispatchers" (101). At other stations, too, reporters "tended to rely on public relations officers and top bureaucrats to warn them about news even though they acknowledged that such officials are unlikely to call public attention to controversies that might show their agency in a negative light" (104–5). The result is obvious: "Passive discovery tends to surrender control over the public information stream to powerful interests in government, large corporations, and among the wealthy" (107), thereby producing news that tends to disseminate consensual beliefs only. When the news is itself provided by business and government, censorship and other forms of self-conscious manipulation are unnecessary for the preservation of dominant ideology.

This sort of structural limitation or exclusion is by no means confined to the news media. It is found, for example, in university English departments, where until recently almost all the authors taught were white and male. This was not because department heads set out to censor women and nonwhite authors, to prevent instructors from teaching these works. Though such censorship no doubt occurred at times (and various sorts of pressure just short of censorship happened with more frequency), the primary reason for the exclusion of women and nonwhites was a matter of the organization of the profession. The listing of courses in catalogs rarely if ever included Africa, India, or the Caribbean, though each region has many anglophone writers. The catalog descriptions of the courses rarely mentioned women's names, though they typically mandated the teaching of a number of male authors. The anthologies available for courses rarely included works by women or nonwhites, and so on.

Again, this sort of structural exclusion tends to be self-perpetuating. Consider literary theory. There were important traditions of literary theory in India, China, Japan, and the Arab world, but these are entirely absent from courses in literary theory. One reason for this is that the texts are not readily available, and not available at all in textbook form. In response to this problem, I tried to convince several publishers to print a collection of non-Western literary theory. Every one of these publishers turned down the project on the grounds that non-Western theory is not taught, so there is no market. In other words, it cannot be taught, at least in part, because there is no textbook. But no one is willing to publish a textbook, in part because it is not taught. There may have been an element of censorship—or of censorshiplike motivation—in the publishers' immediate refusal of the project (that is, there seems to have been more to it than a mere marketing decision), yet it was not merely censorship either. There was a structure in place that tended toward self-perpetuation, independent of the precise nature of alternatives—alternatives that were, then, systemically excluded from consideration.

Beyond lies, censorship, and structural exclusion, obfuscation and certain sorts of metaphorical indirection are also common. Most often, these serve to obscure significant but unpalatable facts. They may also operate to imply false statements. Examples from the Gulf War are legion. As Colin McEnroe (1991) observed, in Pentagon newspeak, "bombing a target" became "acquiring an asset," dead civilians were subsumed under the vaguer category "collateral damage," the killing or wounding of 100,000 Iraqi soldiers became "the degradation of Iraqi military capability by 15 to 20 percent," and so forth. At best, a phrase such as "collateral damage" conceals civilian casualties. At worst, it implies that there were no civilian casualties. One is inclined to feel, after all, that if they meant that civilians were killed, surely they would have said so; since they didn't say that civilians were killed, they must have meant something else. They must have meant that property was damaged—the sort of thing that stands as collateral for a bank loan. They couldn't possibly be referring to people with the term.

The same holds true with metaphors. When George Bush said that the United States must "push Saddam Hussein back" (quoted in Lakoff 1991b), he was employing pushing a single human being as a metaphor for a military attack on an army of hundreds of thousands, and as it turned out, tens of thousands of civilians as well. At best, this metaphor occluded the real destruction of the war. While it was unlikely to foster a self-conscious belief that there had been no such destruction, it encouraged people to imagine the conflict in benign terms. Indeed, this reduction of war to a nonlethal personal struggle was common to a wide range of metaphors regularly used by politicians and journalists. As Jim Naureckas (1991) explained, "Journalists constantly asked, 'How long will it take to defeat Saddam Hussein?' or 'How badly are we hurting him?' as if wars are fought against single individuals, rather than nations. . . . ABC's Ann Compton continued the fiction that the war targeted a single person: 'If Iraq does use chemical weapons [against rebels], it will bring more air attacks down on Saddam Hussein's head" (3).

Many of the same practices that operate to determine specific beliefs may function to establish problematics. The most obvious way in which limits of belief are established is through not reporting alternative views. Some views simply get little or no exposure. This has been facilitated in recent years by changes in the laws governing broadcast media. "Until recently, a policy critic who was denied access to the airwaves could appeal to the Federal Communication Commission on the basis of the Fairness Doctrine, which instructed broadcasters to air diverse views on controversial issues," says Robert Krinsky (1991). "But a Reagan/Bush FCC bent on deregulation suspended the doctrine in 1987."

Though the establishment of a problematic is usually an informal and cumulative process, sometimes the limits of discussion are marked explicitly. Fouad Ajami, who served as a political commentator for CBS, claimed that in the media's coverage of the war, "everyone is being heard: the people who favor this war, the people who think it's a just war are being heard; the people who think it is just barely a just war are being heard; the people who believe Saddam is a hero are getting their airtime from Amman and from the West Bank and so on" (quoted in Naureckas 1991, 4). According to Ajami, there were three possible positions on the war: the allied attack on Iraq was extremely just; the allied attack on Iraq was just, but barely; or Saddam Hussein's attack on Kuwait was just. Thus, the only alternative to supporting the allied bombardment was backing Hussein's aggression. The implication is, if one doesn't support Hussein's attack on Kuwait, then logically one must uphold the allied attack on Iraq. The positions of virtually every member of the peace movement were simply excluded. (Note how this is directly parallel to the exclusion of, say, democratic socialism from the range of alternatives to the present social system. In each case, a clearly objectionable system is established as the only realistic option to the status quo.)

Examples of the same sort may be found in most of the numerous polls conducted during the war. As one Gallup poll asked in February 1991, "Do you think U.S. and allied forces should begin a ground attack soon to drive the Iraqis out of Kuwait—or should we hold off for now and continue to rely on air power to do the job?" (The Polling Game 1991, 11). A ceasefire and negotiations simply were not possibilities according to the problematic defined by this question. Rather, there were two options: ground war or aerial bombardment. Whichever position one might take on this issue, one necessarily consents to the war.

Ellipsis, discourse emphasis, and repetition are the standard modes of producing consent-fostering focalization. As to ellipsis, when Bush denounced the Iraqi annexation of Kuwait, he did not mention the far worse occupations and annexations that had occurred earlier in the region and elsewhere. For instance, he ignored the Israeli occupation of southern Lebanon, Moroccan annexation of the western Sahara, Turkish occupation of northern Cyprus, and Indonesian annexation of East Timor. Neither did the mainstream media cite these cases. The focus of discussion was placed entirely on Iraq. Moreover, here as elsewhere, focalization is bound up with the generation of beliefs. When no comparable cases are mentioned, one's tendency is to assume that none exist, that the annexation of Kuwait was unique and uniquely brutal. In fact, Iraq killed some 700 people when it invaded Kuwait; Israel killed some 20,000 people in southern Lebanon— and received $25 billion in U.S. aid in the next nine years; and Indonesia committed virtual genocide in East Timor, killing 100,000 people, mostly with U.S. weapons (see Media 1991).

By discourse emphasis, I mean the placement of stories, analyses, reports, or crucial information within stories, and so on, such as to draw or divert attentional focus. For example, the day after the 26 January march on Washington in 1991, the *Hartford Courant* ran a front-page story on Hartford Whalers fans waving U.S. flags at a hockey match and included on the same page a large color photo of a "Support the Troops" rally. The brief story on the antiwar march was relegated to page 11. In this case, focalization did not operate to draw scrutiny and criticism but rather to divert attention from criticisms of the war that might encourage scrutiny of U.S. actions and to stress popular support for the war. Note that focalization has this function, independent of the editors' motives. The editors may have been indifferent to popular enthusiasm for the war, wishing merely to avoid criticism from prowar groups. The result is the same. On the other hand, many cases of this sort are entirely self-conscious, as when a company with a poor record of hiring and promoting women or minorities makes a woman or minority executive its official spokesperson to the media.

A technique related to discourse emphasis is repetition: the amount of time or space devoted to one or another topic or claim. While advocates of the war were regularly consulted, interviewed, and quoted, "only about 1.5 percent of network sources were protesters, about the same number as sources asked about how the war had affected their travel plans" (Naureckas 1991, 5). This has much the same focalizing effect as the large, front-page picture of a prowar rally and the minimal, page 11 coverage of the antiwar rally, and serves much the same function. Similarly, a Fairness and Accuracy in Reporting (FAIR) survey showed that the four Israelis killed by Iraqi missiles were given more than three times the media attention accorded the thousands of Iraqi civilians killed by the U.S. bombardment (see Naureckas 1991, 7–8). This clearly focalizes attention on Iraqi crimes, much like the English stress on human sacrifice among the Igbo.

FUNDAMENTAL BELIEFS, CONFIRMATORY BIAS, AND ANCHORING EFFECT

Unsurprisingly, not all ideological beliefs are equally consequential for the development of consent. Perhaps the most ideologically crucial beliefs are those acquired in childhood. Whether they concern the alleged benevolence of U.S. foreign policy, the supposed rationality of males and nurturance of females, the putative inferiority of nonwhites, or the purported identity of personal freedom and market freedom, the consent of adults is to a great extent built on the beliefs learned as children.

More generally, some beliefs are "fundamental" in that they play a definitive and continuing role in the development of a wide range of more "local" beliefs. Most often acquired in childhood, fundamental beliefs are tenacious almost to the point of being ineradicable. They distort people's perceptions and even their memories, reforming individuals' experience in their image. For many years, cognitive scientists have been aware of a broad human tendency to reinterpret experience in conformity with basic beliefs; this is sometimes referred to as "confirmatory bias." This is, in the first place, a universal human tendency spontaneously to class as confirmatory all data that fit one's beliefs, while spontaneously classing disconfirmatory data as "exceptions" (see, for example, Mynatt, Doherty, and Tweney 1977; Mahoney 1977, 161–62; and Nisbett and Ross 1980, 238–42). When one meets an irrational woman or unnurturant man, the tendency is to take these as proof of the stereotypes; when one meets a woman who is lucid and careful in her reasoning or a humanitarian man, the tendency is to class these as exceptions, not as evidence against the stereotype. The same tendency is clear in relation to U.S. foreign policy, racism, and so on.

More generally, confirmatory bias involves the confirmatory reconstrual of neutral—or even prima facie disconfirming—evidence. As Steven Neuberg (1994) points out, "Numerous studies indicate that identical behavior is often perceived differently, depending on the target's group membership; these biases in impressions are often in the direction of confirming the perceiver's stereotype-based expectancies" (107). Richard Nisbett and Lee Ross (1980) give the following example: "The adult black, observed sitting on a park bench at 3 p.m. on a Wednesday might be coded as unemployed, lazy, and probably on welfare, whereas a white observed in similar circumstances would more likely be given the 'benefit of the doubt'; that is, to be coded as enjoying a day off, relaxing before beginning work on the night shift, or even as being the innocent victim of recession layoffs" (240). In one study, groups were presented with sketches of children engaged in different activities. If the child "was black, his [sic] behavior was judged to be more mean and threatening, and less playful and friendly, than if [he] was white." In short, "the same behavioral act was interpreted differently depending on the race of the person who performed it" (Hamilton and Trolier 1986, 143).

This is not all there is to it. Confirmatory bias is so strong that people tend actually to misperceive or misremember particulars if they conflict with strongly held beliefs. Neuberg (1994) notes that "under some circumstances, targets are viewed in an expectancy-consistent manner even when their behavior is objectively inconsistent with the perceivers' expectancies" (107). In one study, for instance, white television viewers "watched a newscast that showed no photo of a suspect." Afterward, "40 percent believed they saw an African American perpetrator" (Douglas 1997b, 19). Worse still, in one famous study, a number of subjects were shown a picture of a group of people in a subway. A white person held a weapon. When asked afterward who was holding the weapon, many of the subjects identified a black as the malefactor (see Loftus 1980, 39), their perception or memory completely twisted by racist beliefs. Indeed, even when an experience is accurately articulated immediately after it has occurred, people have a tendency to misremember it later on, distorting it in memory to conform to their fundamental beliefs (this has been demonstrated in a number of nonpolitical—specifically scientific—contexts [see White 1992, 156, including citations]).

Nisbett and Ross (1980) explain that in general, "perception of covariation in the social domain"—for example, the perception that blacks are lazy—is most often "a function of preexisting theories," including stereotypes (111). They stress that cognitive tendencies such as this are behaviorally consequential. Indeed, people's behavior "sometimes amplifies" these sorts of judgmental errors (11). In my terms, they not only give rise to motivational beliefs but motivational beliefs that appear to be even more absolute than the correlated self-conscious ones. A biased inference that "many" blacks are lazy, for example, may give rise to behavior that tacitly presupposes *most* or *nearly all* blacks are lazy.

It may seem that there is a simple solution to this problem: disseminate the facts. But there are several problems with this. First of all, it is difficult to disseminate nonstandard views at all—for the process of dissemination itself is pervaded by confirmatory bias. As Mahoney (1977) has demonstrated, even in science, it is extremely difficult to publish material that does not fit standard opinions. In one study, Mahoney wrote up two different versions of a psychology experiment. The data in the first version were strongly confirmatory of accepted opinion. In the second version, Mahoney merely reversed the data tables so that they were strongly disconfirmatory of accepted opinion. By intellectual criteria, the second version should have been far more valuable, and thus, far more likely to be published. But, in fact, the opposite occurred—the first version was significantly more likely to be published. Largely because of confirmatory bias, this (intellectually less valuable) confirmatory version was evaluated far more favorably than the (methodologically identical) disconfirmatory version. (For other problems with peer review, see Horrobin 1982; for related problems in the conduct of research, see Faust 1984, 89–92, 99.)

Another significant difficulty with "disseminating the facts" as a solution to confirmatory and related biases results from the nature of fundamental beliefs. Even when people come to accept new beliefs, they do not, most often, abandon their fundamental ones. Rather, they accept and apply the new beliefs in narrow contexts, often through self-conscious decision, while generally living their lives on the basis of the fundamental beliefs.

Contrary to what one might assume, everyone holds contradictory beliefs. And they hold them about a wide range of things—almost everything, in fact. People are not paralyzed by this only because the beliefs have different degrees of saliency and/or motivational force. Frequently, that difference in saliency or motivational force is a function of context. One belief is more salient in one context; another belief is more salient in another context. In the case at hand, the fundamental belief could be conceived of as the default belief, the belief held in general. The new belief comes into play—that is, achieves predominance in saliency or force—only when triggered by particular contextual features. In all other contexts, individuals operate unselfconsciously on the basis of the fundamental (default) belief.

This phenomenon is well established in the area of scientific belief. As a number of researchers have demonstrated, even for advanced students in natural science, "all that straightforward instruction does is place a veneer of scientists' views over the strongly held unscientific beliefs" (White 1992, 155). For example, most people grow to maturity with fundamental beliefs about the physical world that are roughly Aristotelian. In studying physics, people may come to internalize Newtonian or Einsteinian beliefs. They may be able to act on these beliefs, reason via these beliefs, and the like, when they are taking a physics exam or are doing research in physics. But even those who go on to do advanced work in physics rarely substitute the Newtonian or Einsteinian beliefs for the Aristotelian ones. The Aristotelian ones remain fundamental, guiding thought and action in most of life, while the Newtonian or Einsteinian views are "triggered" only by such contexts as that of research or test taking. As Holland et al. (1987) explain, "Strong rules [ideas, beliefs] learned in childhood will not be forgotten or replaced by subsequent learning. Instead, such rules will remain in the system, to be called up when later circumstances resemble those under which the rules were first learned" (354), which is to say, in this case, the circumstances of ordinary life—in contrast to the far more limited context of the classroom or laboratory. Moreover, at any time, the presuppositions of the former may spill over into the latter, leading, for instance, to errors in exams, or even in the design and interpretation of research. In sum, "people reliably distort the new [ideas or beliefs] in the direction of the old ones, or ignore them altogether except in highly specific domains" (206).

Clearly, the discrepancy between fundamental and contextual beliefs is highly consequential outside of academic science. It is no doubt one cause of such phenomena as the U.S. populace's contradictory tendency to assert that politicians are all corrupt and dishonest, and at the same time, to accept unquestioningly much of what politicians actually say. It can be seen in the conformist behavior of rebels, the racist actions (and even remarks) of "antiracists," and so forth. Along with self-interest, it is no doubt one of the reasons for the common tendency of revolutionaries to slip into conformity. In each case, there seems to be a strong, consensual, fundamental belief operating in contradiction with a more recently acquired, nonconsensual belief, with the former asserting itself outside of special contexts or at times when one's self-conscious vigilance flags.

Finally, a broad cognitive tendency related to both confirmatory bias and fundamental belief is what cognitive psychologists refer to as the "anchoring effect." The anchoring effect is the expression of a general human tendency to moderate one's inferences, ideas, and such by reference to preceding instances of the same general type. It is, in effect, a principle of cognitive conformism, whereby any relevant idea or action will serve to anchor subsequent ideas or actions of the same sort. Suppose five people are asked to estimate the price of a car. The first person's estimate will serve to anchor all the others in that it will provide a sort of base from which they will operate. Put differently, whatever their initial impulse might be, they will readjust their estimate to bring it more in line with the first one.

This sounds reasonable enough when it is a question of pricing an automobile. But this tendency extends to all areas and is entirely automatic. In one study, people were asked to estimate various percentages, such as the percentage of African countries in the United Nations. Before giving their answers, they watched their questioner spin a wheel marked with numbers from 1 to 100. After the wheel stopped, the test subjects were asked to give their estimates. Despite the fact that the number shown on the wheel was generated entirely at random, it still had the effect of anchoring estimates. When the number on the wheel was higher, the subjects' estimates were higher; when it was lower, theirs were lower, too (Tversky and Kahneman 1977, 335–36). The same holds for any sort of evaluation, approximation, or inference. If five people are on a committee, evaluating a grant proposal or tenure candidate, the first opinion uttered is likely to serve as a base for subsequent deliberation.

When transferred to politically significant concerns, it should be immediately apparent that the consequences of the anchoring effect will almost invariably be consensual. In effect, dominant ideology always has the first word, and so, establishes a basis for other opinions. This is not true in some mystical sense but quite concretely. The U.S. government is likely to give the first word on any policy of national or international note. That first word will be broadcast throughout the nation, even the world, making it the base for almost everyone's understanding of the policy in question. When the U.S. government said that the only possible response to the Iraqi invasion of Kuwait was military punishment, this served to anchor all subsequent responses, even for the Left. Prior to the government's statement, the Left's response might have been something like "Let's just not bother about Iraq/Kuwait, and instead concentrate our energies on, say, East Timor, Lebanon, or the western Sahara." But after the government pronouncement, even the Left shifted to advocating a boycott. (I am not saying that the Left was wrong, just that it probably would not have even considered a boycott had it not been for the anchoring effect of the U.S. government position.)

The same point holds in the debate over welfare. When prominent Republican senators or representatives followed Ronald Reagan in insisting that welfare enriches a profligate group of lazy and shiftless men and women, this anchored subsequent debate in obvious ways. More concretely, consider the debate in California over benefits. Governor Pete Wilson articulated a particularly harsh plan, eliminating benefits after one year, reducing them after six months, and more. As one writer put it, "Wilson no doubt staked out such an extreme position on welfare so that any eventual compromise would seem moderate by comparison" (Wilson's War 1997, 11). Whether Wilson set out with this intention or not (perhaps he genuinely advocated the extreme measures he proposed), his statement had the anchoring effect one would expect. Here, it combined with federal law to define a problematic. An editorial in the *San Francisco Chronicle* maintained that the true path to so-called welfare reform lay "between Wilson's mean-spirited approach and the Democrats' overly lenient path"—this "overly lenient path" being "Sen. Diane Watson's proposed legislation allowing recipients to receive benefits for the full five years allowed under federal law" (quoted in ibid.). The anchoring effect of Wilson's proposal was strong enough to exclude any option to the left of federal law, and thus, any debate over federal welfare policy—other than debate over whether it was overly lenient. By way of contrast, consider how different the debate would have been had it begun with the assertion that inflexible mandates of this sort will deepen poverty, extend unemployment, and harm everyone, and that people should therefore look for legal ways to extend support beyond five years as needed.

INHIBITORY METABELIEFS: IDEOLOGICAL
SELF-CRITICISM AND DESPAIR

As several of the preceding examples indicate, consent on a given issue is affected by many beliefs that do not directly concern that issue per se. Popular consent to the Gulf War was, in part, based on beliefs about the Vietnam War and U.S. foreign policy in general. Other types of indirect belief are crucial also—as we shall discuss in the next section, part of popular consent to the Gulf War was based on beliefs about expertise. One belief of particular importance for consent in a wide range of cases is that one is alone or nearly alone in questioning standard views. As Noam Chomsky (1991) has argued, "If you take particular programs like armaments or cutting back on social spending and so on, almost every one of them was unpopular." Nevertheless, "people who answered in polls 'I'd prefer social spending to military spending'—as people overwhelming did—assumed that they were the only people with that crazy idea in their heads because they never heard it anywhere else." As a result, they "feel like an oddity" (ibid.). The consensual effects of this are clear. It is difficult to maintain confidence in one's own judgment when absolutely everyone else appears to have come to precisely the opposite conclusion.

Returning to the Gulf War, while there was not widespread opposition to it, there was far more significant opposition than was reported in the mainstream media. People who might have questioned the justification of the war were strongly discouraged from doing so by the portrayal of protesters as a tiny, fringe element. Minor examples could be seen in various reports on local antiwar rallies. A striking case may be found in the New York Times report on the national antiwar rally in Washington on 19 January 1991. This article numbered the crowd at 15,000—10,000 fewer than the police count of 25,000, and 60,000 fewer than the organizers' count of 75,000 (see Anti-Anti-War Coverage 1991, 19). Worse still, "in the first five months of the Gulf crisis, only about one percent of the coverage on the three nightly network news programs dealt, even tangentially, with popular opposition to Bush administration policy" (ibid.). According to Los Angeles Times television critic Howard Rosenberg, the ABC affiliate in Los Angeles unofficially banned coverage of peace demonstrations (Cleared by Self-Censors? 1994). There was a similar misrepresentation of the international scene, with little attention paid to the ways in which members of the UN Security Council were manipulated and even bribed into supporting belligerence (see, for example, Weir 1991, 15).

In such circumstances, it is unsurprising that most people found the justice of the war unquestionable. People were not necessarily simply being conformist; here as elsewhere, that was an important factor, but that was not all there was to it. Even independent-minded people are and should be inclined to criticize the conclusions of their own thought. The fact that everyone else has come to a different conclusion is often good reason to think that one is wrong. If someone had a momentary hesitation, a question about the justice of the war, and then saw that many people felt the same way, he or she might develop a fully critical attitude because his or her initial hesitation or question would appear reasonable. Yet when virtually everyone else seemed to find the justice of the war beyond doubt, such a person was likely to assume that his or her hesitation or question was misplaced. If one works an algebra problem and comes up with one answer, but the teacher and all the other students come up with another result, it is not merely sheepishly conformist to assume that one is wrong; it is reasonable self-criticism.

This ideological self-criticism may be understood as a sort of "inhibitory metabelief": a belief that may or may not undermine one's dissident beliefs but that in any case inhibits one's full commitment to, development of, and action on those beliefs. A second inhibitory metabelief that is particularly crucial for consensual ideology is aimed not at oneself and the validity of one's own beliefs but at the social world and the possibility of implementing one's beliefs. Even when one does not accept the problematic that categorizes as utopian all superior alternatives to the current social structure, one may easily come to believe that changing the current structure is impossible in practice. In other words, one might in principle accept that a better society could exist, that it is not somehow excluded as a result of, say, human nature. Still, one might be unable to see any practical activity that will help to move society in that direction. One may succumb to a sort of political despair, a feeling that political action is simply hopeless given the current circumstances. Despair is probably most common among those who strongly feel the need for social change—most obviously, those who are particularly brutalized by the system (for example, the most immiserated 20 percent)—but who also feel entirely alone, unconnected with others who share their views and commitments. Such despair is a recurring theme in the literature of European colonies: for instance, in Things Fall Apart, Chinua Achebe's Okonkwo commits suicide when he sees no hope for the Igbo in resisting complete subordination to the British, when he looks about his society and finds no one but himself with the will to resist.

Marxists have long recognized such despair as a particular danger to any progressive movement and have stressed the importance of solidarity as a response. It is through joining with others in collective struggle that oppressed people begin to sense their strength and gain the confidence needed to fend off despair. This is also the reason why some marxist literary critics have insisted that literature should not be tragic only but should hold out hope for future struggle. Literary works should not pretend that there are no difficulties, that liberation will be easy. But they should make clear that these difficulties are not insuperable, that it is possible to overcome them through group action. I am not sure how much difference literature makes in this regard, yet it does seem clear that individuals are less likely to fall into political despair if they are joined with others in collective struggle. Indeed, it seems less probable that they will fall into those forms of personal despair that have obvious political roots—the despair caused by unemployment (see Cohen and Rogers 1983, 29), by the realization that one is gay (Heinze [1995] points out that the suicide rate for young gays and lesbians is several times greater than average [9]), and so on. Despair concerns the possibility of real change, in society as well as one's own life, and is bound up with a sense of alienation from others. As such, it is, in the first place, acts of solidarity that dissipate despair; and it is the absence of solidarity that makes despair so thick as to suffocate not only action but, in the most extreme and tragic cases, even the ordinary will to live.

THE CREATION OF EXPERTISE AND THE PACIFYING FUNCTION OF CONSULTATION

Having considered the content of beliefs, and the relation of beliefs to one another, it is important to take up the ideological definition of authority—the expertise granted to those who disseminate ideological beliefs—as well as the interaction between those who articulate consensual ideology and those who accept it. For these do not merely provide a context for consensual ideology; they are a crucial part of it, too.

One of the central methods for fostering beliefs, defining problematics, and creating focalization is the establishment of expertise. After all, it is experts or authorities who set up the poles of debate, focus on the topics of primary attention, and the like. This is true equally of the political experts interviewed on *Nightline* and the academic experts whose articles appear in the most prestigious journals.

The first thing to note about authority is that what comes to count as expertise in any given system will be a function of hierarchies of domination. This is true for the simple reason that those who are assigned the systemic role of authorities (news anchors, policy analysts, and so on), are those who have succeeded in some systemic hierarchy. And those who have succeeded will, on the whole, be those who act in accordance with the principles of that hierarchy. This is so even in supposedly pure intellectual meritocracies, such as the university, as indicated, for example, by Michael Mahoney's (1977) research on the strong confirmatory bias of scholarly publication. As already mentioned, his research shows that work supporting standard views is significantly more likely to be published than methodologically identical work disputing standard views (see Hogan 1993). This—effectively consensual—establishment of authority will only be more prominent in explicitly political systems, in corporations (including corporate news media), and so on. There are, of course, exceptions. But the tendency is almost inevitable, and unsurprisingly so.

To make matters worse, any dissidents from standard views who do manage to achieve some level of institutional authority are rarely given any public forum. They do not function as experts in the most consequential ways. For example, they are virtually excluded from the mainstream media, in discussions of U.S. foreign policy, cognition and gender, affirmative action, or whatever. As Edward Herman and Noam Chomsky (1988) remark, the vast majority of "experts" appearing in mainstream media are government officials, former government officials, or members of conservative think tanks (for instance, almost 70 percent on the *McNeil-Lehrer News Hour*, 25).

Those dissident voices that do make their way into the media are typically presented in such a way as to deny any authority to the views. Naureckas (1991) points out that during the Gulf crisis, "when anti-war voices were heard, it was very rarely as in-studio guests partaking in substantive discussions" (5). Rather, antiwar views were typically confined to brief interviews with ordinary individuals participating in antiwar rallies. "Relying, as network TV did, on random protesters to present a movement's views is to deny that movement its most articulate and knowledgeable spokespeople. The situation is comparable to depending on interviews with the crowd at a Republican rally to convey the views of the Bush administration" (ibid.). Indeed, "a survey conducted by FAIR of the sources on the ABC, CBS, and NBC nightly news found that of 878 on-air sources, only one was a representative of a national peace organization—Bill Monning of Physicians Against Nuclear War. By contrast, seven players from the Super Bowl were brought on to comment on the war" (ibid.).

The situation is similar across the board. For example, the same principles apply to politically consequential academic science—witness the ease with which the shoddiest research claiming gender or race difference can gain national media attention (see Faludi's [1991] discussions of the former).

Finally, the recognized experts operate not only to disseminate beliefs; they also perpetuate the system of expertise, and deepen the division between experts and ordinary people. In some ways, the ideal expert is one who never has to explain anything, who has convinced people that his or her topic is so recondite, or so politically nuanced, that it simply cannot be made comprehensible to nonexperts. If this is accomplished, the reaction of the populace can only be something like, "Well, they're the experts. I suppose they know what they are doing. It's beyond me."

This is obviously true in academic disciplines, including areas of research that are politically and socially important (such as race and intelligence). It is also true in political discourse. During the Gulf War, the air of technical expertise surrounding the obscure language of governmental spokespersons tended not only to occlude unsavory facts, as discussed above, but to establish those spokespersons as authorities with sophistication well beyond that of average people. It is difficult to think of oneself as competent to question the decisions of officials when one does not even comprehend the terms of the debate. The inclination is to think that special training is required, that the average person can no more have a rational view on the "degradation of military capability" than on the nature of quarks.

Or consider the economic analyses offered by different political authorities to justify such policies as cutting social benefits or giving more money to big business. A good example is provided by the proposals put forth in the report of the Advisory Council on Social Security. These would affect every U.S. citizen. Yet one political commentator wrote that the report is "so complicated, technical, and jargon-laden that it makes your average computer-instruction manual look like a comic book" (Douglas 1997a, 19). Despite its universal impact, almost no one is likely to feel capable of evaluating this report or its proposals.

In short, the system of expertise operates not only to foster consensual beliefs about particular actions or events, such as the Gulf War, and confine debate on those issues within a narrow problematic. It also encourages the more general perception that judgments about politically consequential situations require inaccessible technical knowledge. Largely by means of this view, it promotes a broad, content-neutral deference to authority. This, in turn, tends to encourage a passive attitude toward politics, where citizens leave political life in the hands of the experts, implicitly trusting their decisions. In the most extreme case, the citizenry does not consent to individual policies or practices as such, but in effect, to whatever the authorities decide. Indeed, this stance was frequently articulated by ordinary people interviewed during the Gulf War: "It's not up to us to say the war is wrong," explained one interviewee (Rallies 1991, A6).

On the other hand, this does not mean that people feel they should not be consulted. Indeed, consultation complements and completes expertise; it makes expertise "democratic," or at least buttresses the perception that it does not contradict, but incorporate, democracy. Though further research is no doubt in order, some early studies indicate that people are more likely to be satisfied with, say, a social structure or government policy if they feel the government has considered their opinions—even if government policy runs counter to those opinions, and to those people's interests. As Michael Baer and Dean Jaros (1974) summarize it, "Though individual participation may have little direct consequence for substantive policy output, it may be of tremendous import in the level of disaffection in—and therefore the stability of—political systems" (365). In other words, if people believe that their opinion has been taken into consideration, they are far more likely to consent to government policies, even if the policies show no effect of this consideration.

The entire operation of democracy under capitalism clearly functions to encourage the belief that the political system incorporates the views of citizens, most obviously through elections. These elections, however, are at best processes of elite decision and popular ratification, as Chomsky (1987) has argued (24). A number of writers have stressed that capitalist democracy is structured in such a way as to confine policy formulation to a narrowly class-based group. This is true in two senses: the members of government are predominantly bourgeois (see, for example, Nader 1982), and nongovernmental members of the moneyed classes have access to and influence on members of government, the outcome of elections, and the like, to a degree proportionate not to their numbers but their economic status (as discussed in my introduction). In elections, members of all classes do have a voice. Nevertheless, with rare exceptions, they are only able to choose from a set of options already formulated by members of the elite, options most often limited by a narrow problematic (for a striking example of this—the virtual identity of Eugene McCarthy's and Richard Nixon's views on the Vietnam War, despite their different rhetoric—see Anker, Seybold, and Schwartz 1987, 100).

Thus, the form of the system—as well as the rhetoric of politicians, lessons learned in grammar school civics classes, etc.—facilitates the view that the opinions of ordinary people count, even though the system in fact allows virtually no room for those opinions, no scope for their articulation, no possibility for their implementation.

Most people, of course, probably recognize that their opinions do not have any real effects. That is exactly the point. The pacifying effect is produced by the mere fact that people can vote in elections, that they can write to their representatives and receive replies, that government officials appear to pay attention to the results of opinion polls (which are themselves seen as representing the views of the people, even though these results are largely a residue of the way the polls have prestructured relevant problematics). In short, the pacifying, and thus consensual, effect is produced by people's sense that their opinions have been "considered" by the authorities. This is part of what allows people to accept them as authorities. Individuals can grant them both expertise and authority over their lives, thereby more readily consenting to their judgments, insofar as the authorities' decisions are based not only on private knowledge but "take into account" the views of a wide range of other people, of the citizenry in general. Again, this is true even if the actions of the authorities do not evidence any practical influence of the views supposedly taken into account.

THREE   *Ideology and Emotion*

The emotive factors in ideological consent are clearly extensive. I have already touched on some in connection with self-interest, desire, and despair. This chapter will focus on what are probably the two most ideologically consequential types of affective attitude. In psychoanalytic terms, these are "narcissism" and "transference," and they are closely related to what social psychologists refer to "ingroup" and "outgroup" relations. The first case deals with those forms of emotion and cognition in which a subject sees someone else as a sort of version of him or herself. The second case deals with those forms of emotion and cognition in which a subject sees someone else as definitively different from and even opposed to him or herself. The former is based on identification, while the latter is expressed in an "object attitude," such as love, hate, admiration, or envy.

More exactly, when someone consents to war, racial oppression, a sexual division of labor, or an economic hierarchy, he or she feels something about the people involved. One may identify with other people—not merely in the sense of seeing that particular interests coincide but in feeling a nonrational joy in their individual or collective successes or sorrow in their failures, independent of the effect such successes and failures might have on one's own life. On the other hand, one may feel disgust (such as for gay men), loathing (for Arabs, for instance), or sentimental affection (perhaps for women). These feelings are just as important as one's beliefs in determining whether or not one consents to a given social structure, policy, or whatever.

Identification may be interpreted, first of all, as a function of self-conception. People understand themselves—much as they understand other people or material objects—in terms of a hierarchy of properties and relations. For example, I am male, have blue eyes, and wear brown pants. I have all these properties. But in my self-conception, I am more centrally male than blue eyed, more centrally blue eyed than wearing brown pants. Identification may be seen as an affective attachment to another person or persons insofar as they share certain properties with me that are key to my self-understanding, properties that are high in my hierarchized self-concept (for research on this in a literary context, see Klementz-Belgardt 1981, 367–68, including the citations). Thus I am, in general, more likely to identify with men than with people wearing brown pants.

Gender, race, and ethnicity are some of the properties most commonly privileged in self-definition, and thus, some of the properties most commonly determinative of identification. Moreover, they are the most socially consequential properties of this type. I will refer to them as "essential." This is not, of course, because they really do isolate a genuinely definitive aspect of one's being. Rather, it is because they are widely understood—self-consciously and motivationally—as definitive. Though these properties may be acknowledged as being open to alteration, they nonetheless tend to be conceived of as permanent, as both intrinsic and constant. In other words, people tend to see them simply as part of what they are, such that if these properties changed, a person's identity would change also. As well, people tend to see them as not varying, not shifting with circumstances, and so on. I do not think of myself as male in one context and female in another.

Contrast this to properties related to employment. These do not operate as essential properties, since they are not conceived of as permanent. If Smith is a white male factory worker, he is likely to find it unimaginable that he would be "the same person" if he were to become black or female. Yet there is no such problem with respect to his being a factory worker. He may well believe that it is practically impossible that he would ever, say, start his own business. But imagining such a development does not contradict his sense of identity. Similarly, being fired from his job might be devastating for him. But "unemployed Smith" is unlikely to be a conceptual anomaly for him, in the way, say, "female Smith" would be.

Obviously, the conception of identity is fuzzy here. But that is necessary, because Smith's own conception of identity is likely to be fuzzy. For our purposes, all that matters is that Smith would imagine some changes to be disruptive of his personal identity and others not. Note also that this imagination of identity has no bearing on actual consequences of real change. Suppose Smith discovers that he is not an English Anglican, as he had always thought. Instead, he is the child of Pakistani Muslims, a group that he had always loathed and seen as the antithesis of his own. In fact, this may result in far less dislocation in his sense of self or general emotional well-being than getting fired from his job, even though he previously imagined his ethnicity to be essential. The point is not that, say, ethnicity really is one of the most psychologically consequential properties of Smith, but rather that Smith is likely to conceive of it that way, and to act on that conception.

This already has direct ideological consequences. The fact that race, for example, is conceived of as essential while employment is categorized as contingent means that people will be predisposed to identify with others based on race and not employment. While solidarity is not simply a matter of feeling identification, it is clearly aided and advanced by such feeling. Moreover, solidarity can be undermined if it runs counter to identification. Marxist theorists have frequently commented that it is remarkably easy to divide members of the working class by race, sex, and ethnicity. In part, this is a matter of microhierarchization, as discussed above. It is also a matter of the psychological structure of identification, however. It is always easier to foster identification based on essential as opposed to nonessential or "contingent" properties—on sex or race, rather than economic class.

Note that this is partly a matter of the properties themselves. Many are simply not good candidates for essences. To be a good candidate, in this sense, a property should generally be salient and, even more important, enduring. Employment status is neither. Its obvious alterability in particular makes it almost impossible to categorize as essential. Sex and skin pigmentation, in contrast, are extremely good candidates, both in saliency and durability.

On the other hand, something does not become an essential property on its own but rather, only when it is rendered broadly socially functional. Consider two other properties likely to count as intrinsic and constant: height and handedness. I do not know of any data on these, yet my conjecture would be that height and handedness almost never count as essential (that is, almost no one in the United States today would find it anomalous to imagine him or herself with a different height or the opposite handedness). The same could just as easily have been true of race, for example. But it is not. Why? Because race is broadly functionalized in society.

Among essentialized categories, sex appears to have a unique place. Some feminists have argued that sexual oppression is the earliest form of oppression, and the model for other forms. In any case, sexual hierarchization does appear to be the most widespread type of social division based on essential properties. It seems, moreover, to have a special cognitive position in people's conception of essence-based stratification (for instance, it enters into conceptualizations of race). This is precisely the outcome one would expect from what has just been said, in that sex is enduring, salient, and from the beginning, socially functional—for sex differences are, after all, crucial to reproduction. This is not to say that sex has to be functionalized in a division of labor or stratification of political power. This is merely to say that since sex (unlike, say, race) *necessarily* has significant and widespread social consequences, it is likely to be essentialized in any society.

As the preceding statement indicates, a socially functionalized property is not of merely local importance. It is not a matter of narrow and unusual circumstances. Rather, a functionalized property is one that has systematic consequences for the distribution of social goods and opportunities. This typically involves the extension of the property in question outside of those activities to which it is directly and necessarily germane (such as from breast feeding to child rearing more generally). An essentialized property is the most extreme form of this—one tacitly understood and acted on as *relevant in all circumstances*. Most properties are considered relevant only in specific contexts. Height, for one, is relevant to playing basketball or having certain roles in a drama, but it is not relevant to being a nurse or doctor, taking a mathematics class, and the like. In principle, the same should be true of sex, race, ethnicity, religion, nationality, and so on. For example, sex is relevant to sexual desire and reproduction, but it should not be relevant to being a nurse or doctor, or to taking a mathematics class. Most people believe it is relevant, though—even most of those who believe that they believe it is not relevant (that is, most people have a motivational belief of this sort, even most of those whose self-conscious belief is the opposite).

That putatively universal relevance is what makes sex "essential," and thus crucial to identification.

But these essentialized properties are not the most basic or definitive ones for humans. The most basic is subjectivity, one's existence as a thinking, feeling person. To lose this subjectivity is to lose one's identity entirely. All identification is, then, necessarily based on a sense of shared subjectivity. I will use the phrase "narcissistic identification" to refer to identifications based on sex, race, and other presumptively essential properties that are narrower than subjectivity. Consent is fostered by the encouragement of narcissistic identification and the discouragement of the broader identification by subjectivity alone. For identification by subjectivity alone would push against stratification. More precisely, in cases where the social structure involves the systematic degradation and suffering of many people (such as blacks or women), consent is often partially contingent on the denial or diminishing of the subjectivity of those people. This, in turn, operates to inhibit identification.

Perhaps the simplest way to undermine such identification is through indirect dehumanization: simply avoiding any statements that would serve to recall the subjectivity of the enemy, underclass, or whomever. There were many examples of this during the Gulf War. For instance, this was one effect of the obscurity of the war briefings. One reason for referring to "collateral damage" rather than "dead civilians" is that the latter phrase foregrounds subjectivity and thus encourages identification. Similarly, due to the paucity of reporters in Iraq, media viewers rarely saw dead Iraqi civilians. More commonly, people's images of the war were built up from night photographs of such things as targeted buildings or computer-generated schematics of smart bombs—representations that necessarily obscured the humanity of the people targeted and bombed.

More direct denial of subjectivity is common as well, and was also much in evidence during the Gulf War. Saddam Hussein, so often a synecdoche for the people of Iraq, was repeatedly characterized as an animal—a dog, a snake—or as insane, and hence, lacking identifiable subjectivity. The Iraqi people themselves were repeatedly depicted as subhuman or deranged. Iraqi troops were referred to as ants, insects, or fish in a barrel. Holly Sklar (1991) reported that "a U.S. pilot described knocking out Iraqi tanks along the Kuwaiti border this way: 'It's almost like you flipped on the light in the kitchen late at night and the cockroaches started scurrying, and we're killing them' " (60; see also Soloman 4). As to insanity, beyond the general portrayals of Muslims as lunatics, there were also more specific references to the Iraqi people. For example, I saw a comedian do a routine in which he gave different countries the names of rock groups. He held up a map of Iraq at one point and announced, "Ten Thousand Maniacs."

As these instances already suggest, the premise for explicit attempts to undermine subjectivity-based identification is invariably intergroup difference—the claim that Europeans are like this, but Arabs or Africans are like that; that men are like this, but women are like that. Teun van Dijk's (1987) research indicates that the most fundamental and common assertion of racism is "They are different" (67; unlike the past, this claim is now more often cultural than biological—see Essed 1991, 14, 248).

On the other hand, the precise nature of this division, the precise terms in which the difference is defined, is obviously relevant as well. While identification is partly a mere formal matter—a matter of categorizing oneself and the other person as "the same"—it is also a matter of vicarious thought and feeling. When people identify with someone, they mentally run though the sorts of ideas, plans, and feelings that they imagine run through the other person's mind. This is much the same process as when people are faced with some hypothetical situation. Suppose a close friend, Smith, receives a demeaning letter from his or her departmental tenure committee, and I am given a copy of the letter. If I identify with Smith, then in reading the letter, I will spontaneously feel stabs of pain, intimations of despair, moments of anger; I will imagine possibilities for response (to the letter's claims about scholarship or teaching) and so on—all according to my general understanding of Smith.

As the discussion thus far may have appeared somewhat pessimistic about solidarity, it is worth dwelling for a moment on identification of this subjective empathic variety. At first it may seem odd that one can identify with others at all. It may appear that people experience themselves directly, and so, to genuinely "sym-pathize" or "suffer with" anyone else would be impossible. How, after all, could anyone "indirectly," "vicariously," or "empathically" feel what someone else feels? In fact, the human mind operates in such a way as to make this sort of fellow feeling quite common. Research indicates that this sort of "parallel" emotion extending from one person to another is achievable even by a simple decision to "adopt the perspective" of the other person (see Davis 1994, 124–25). Moreover, as

Mark Davis explains, "instructions to imagine the affective state of a target frequently trigger a process which ends in the offering of help to that target" (145), or at least aids in "inhibit[ing] aggressiveness" (162).

This may seem anomalous as individuals do not have direct access to the minds of others. But people do not have direct access to their own feelings, ideas, reactions, and so forth, except immediately at the moment they are experiencing them—and even then self-knowledge is limited. As such, people have to infer the causes of their own emotional and other reactions (see Nisbett and Ross 1980, 226–27). Sometimes this is easy (if I am depressed after losing my job, the cause is obvious), but sometimes it is not ("I've been depressed all week, although I'm not sure why"). Moreover, practical planning and decision making, as well as nonpractical fantasy, rely on an ability to project one's own feelings, reactions, and such into hypothetical situations. In short, individuals are faced every day with the problem of understanding their own current feelings and reactions, and imagining their own feelings and reactions in different—hypothetical or expected—circumstances. That problem is almost exactly the same as understanding, imagining, projecting, and identifying with other people's feelings and reactions. To identify empathically with other people is only to engage in a variant of the sort of thing one does with oneself all the time.

Of course, just how self-projection occurs is not easy to explain. One possibility is something like the following. First, a person's cognitive apparatus involves the accessing and application of schemas. These schemas may be broadly divided into "procedural" schemas that guide processes of thought or action, and "representational" ones that provide representational content. The procedural schema for riding a bicycle is not some representation of a bicycle or what riding a bicycle would involve. It is not an object of thought at all. Rather, it is a structured capacity to act, thereby allowing one to ride a bicycle without having to reflect on the process. Procedural schemas clearly incorporate representational schemas. For example, the procedural schema for riding a bicycle would involve the representational schema of a bicycle, for that allows people to recognize a bicycle when they see one.

The projection of oneself into different situations is a function of some sort of procedural schema, along with representational schemas, of others and oneself. Note that even in most *egocentric* cases, projection involves imagining other people's feelings and reactions as well as one's own.

Suppose, for example, I have received a negative tenure letter and am envisioning possible responses, including an interview with the dean's council. Insofar as I am doing this realistically, I need to take into account the likely actions and reactions of the council, and myself in interaction with them, primarily by drawing on the representational schemas just mentioned. What distinguishes the schema of me from those of others in this context is not so much differences in knowledge, for all these cases involve inference and hypothesis. The primary difference is that my self-schema provides the point of view for the scenario. In other words, it is given attentional focus and defines the relevance of outcomes. In projecting a scenario from my own perspective, I focus attention on myself and execute the procedural schema in such a way as to follow through just those outcomes relevant to me. Thus, I try to imagine whether a particular action might convince the dean to award me tenure. I do not try to visualize, say, consequences for the dean's life outside of my situation. In part, empathic identification is merely a variation on this. It is a matter of shifting the point of view—that is, running a procedural schema such that the representation of someone else receives attentional focus and defines the relevance of imagined outcomes.

To return to the notion of dehumanization, in many cases, my only representational schema of other people is one of bare subjectivity. If the humanity of an oppressed group is entirely obscured (by such phrases, for instance, as "collateral damage"), there will not be any representational schemas of other people when I run relevant procedural schemas. When I "imagine" the Gulf War, I may have representational schemas of human U.S. pilots, but not of human Iraqi soldiers or civilians. For example, I may imagine buildings collapsing, but without any people in them. This is not to say that I would explicitly assert there were no people in the buildings. But when I run a hypothetical schema of the bombing in my mind, that procedural schema will incorporate representational ones of U.S. pilots doing the bombing, without any representational schemas of Iraqi people. Put differently, there are U.S. schemas that can serve to define a point of view. In a Walter Mitty–like scenario, I can identify with the pilot, bravely entering Iraqi air space, deftly avoiding enemy fire, bearing in on the "asset." Yet there is no representational schema of an Iraqi woman, holding her two children, wondering whether to flee the building as she hears the planes approach, feeling the panic as the bombs explode and the building collapses around her.

In the case where Iraqi humanity is directly undermined (rather than obscured), I may have representational schemas, yet they are likely to be bestial or insectlike, nonhuman ciphers that cannot serve to define a perspective. Or if they are human, they are rendered dysfunctional through claims of difference.

Specifically, the content of ideological assertions concerning hierarchized group difference is fairly constant and contributes directly to dehumanization. Members of the dominant group (men, whites, Europeans, straights) are characterized as rational, methodical, and restrained, while members of the dominated group (women, blacks, Arabs, gays) are depicted as irrational, emotional, and hysterical. One way of discouraging identification is by presenting the thought processes of the opposed or oppressed group as inscrutable, most often due to inconsistency or even insanity. If another person's thought processes are incomprehensible, if he or she is unpredictable in thought or feeling or action, one simply cannot invoke any representational schema in his or her regard. Even the bare schema of human subjectivity assumes a commonality of reaction to pain, disappointment, or insult; it assumes a similarity in aspiration, desire, and moral principle. Even the bare schema of human subjectivity involves structure and predictability. To make the Other incomprehensibly different is, in effect, to make him or her inhuman, by making his or her feelings and ideas merely random. The situation is only made worse when that other person is viewed as duplicitous as well—a further racist and sexist commonplace. To take one example from the Gulf War, in U.S. *News and World Report*, Judith Kipper maintained that, "We go in a straight line; [Arabs] zig-zag." More exactly, "They can say one thing in the morning, another thing at night and really mean a third thing" (quoted in Naureckas 1991, 9). The similar sexist clichés about female illogic are too well known to require repetition.

GROUP HIERARCHY, SELF-ESTEEM, AND TRAUMA

As these illustrations reveal, ideologically functional identification, or narcissistic identification, is not purely subjective and humanly encompassing but oppositional. Narcissistic identification necessarily involves not only links with one group of people but the denial of links with the complement of that group. For example, to identify oneself narcissistically as white is to see oneself as (emphatically) *not black*. This sort of identification, furthermore, is bound up with a wide range of oppositionally defined judgments and evaluations, concerning such things as intellectual or moral capacities, civil rights, and such. Thus, the systematic development of narcissistic identification serves to foster consent by undermining identification with members of oppressed groups, including those members of one's own oppressed group (say, workers) who are racially or sexually different. In connection with this, it also functions to give narcissistic meaning, and hence emotive force, to particular beliefs and desires that are independently consent inducing. If whites did not define themselves in narcissistic opposition to blacks, for instance, racist beliefs about black intellectual capacities would have far less affective power, and as such, less social effect.

Narcissistic identification is equivalent to what social psychologists refer to as ingroup identification. This is necessarily oppositional, since the ingroup is, by definition, opposed to an outgroup. Ingroup/outgroup divisions appear to be found in all societies and at all times. Perhaps the most fundamental of these divisions is that between the society itself and those outside the society—as in Greeks versus barbarians. This is a particularly easy division to reshape, toward oppressive ends, through dehumanization and the denial of subjectivity. "The anthropologist Robert Redfield has argued that the worldview of many peoples consists essentially of two pairs of binary oppositions: human/nonhuman and we/they. These two are often correlated, as Jonathan Z. Smith observes, so that 'we' equals 'human' and 'they' equals 'not human' " (Pagels 1995, xviii). The case of the United States and Iraq is an obvious instance.

But ingroup/outgroup distinctions are by no means confined to that between the home and alien societies, or even to groups with obvious cultural or other differences. Any group division can give rise to narcissistic identification, even when it is based on nonsalient and changeable properties. Indeed, once an ingroup/outgroup distinction is established—even if arbitrarily—people tend to understand it as quasi-essential, expanding its relevance to all areas of thought and action. As John H. Duckitt (1992) describes it, "Individuals who are categorized into groups will exaggerate their similarity to fellow ingroup members and the dissimilarity of ingroup members to outgroup members, and this will occur on dimensions other than the criterion for categorization" (81). In keeping with this, when ingroup/outgroup distinctions are elaborated, there is a cognitive tendency to understand members of outgroups "as relatively less complex, less variable, and less individuated" than members of ingroups (ibid.)—in short, as less human.

Here, the treatment of human cognition needs to be made a little more complex. Human thought is not guided by broad structures of properties and relations (that is, schemas) alone, or even primarily, but by prototypes also. A prototype may be understood as the "most standard" case of a certain broad category (compare Johnson-Laird and Wason 1977, 342). Consider the concept "bird." In part, birds are conceived of according to a broad schema that involves such properties as "has wings," "has a beak," "lays eggs," and so on. This does not mean that all birds are equally conceived of as birdlike. Nor does it mean that one's recognition of birds, understanding of any reference to birds, or imagination of birds treats all birds equally. In fact, birds tend to be recognized, understood, and imagined in relation to prototypes, not bare definitions. Thus, robins, sparrows, and jays are conceived of as more *prototypical* birds than eagles; and eagles are considered to be more prototypical than vultures; and vultures are seen as more prototypical than penguins. To take a simple case, if someone says, "There are lots of birds at the window," one expects sparrows and robins, not eagles. Indeed, even the schema for "bird" is not a mere listing of necessary and sufficient conditions but incorporates properties of the prototypical birds as "default" cases. For example, the default schema for birds would include "flies," even though that does not apply to, say, penguins. Insofar as one is dealing with a nonprototypical bird, one tends not to think of it, in the first place, as a bird at all; it is not understood by activating the "bird" schema. Rather, it is perceived more specifically, as a "vulture" or "penguin," activating those "lower-level" schemas. Hence, to return to the preceding example, if someone sees robins at the window, it is reasonable for him or her to refer to them as "birds," but if he or she sees eagles, it is probable that he or she will say "eagles."

This procedure—of understanding categories by reference to prototypes and default cases—often makes a good deal of sense. When extended broadly to humans, however, it can have unfortunate ideological consequences. There is a tendency to think of humans not only schematically but prototypically as well. In other words, some types of people are thought of as prototypically human, others as less so, and others as hardly human at all. An understanding of humans operates along the same lines as an understanding of birds, with the same sort of hierarchization of proto-typicality. In this case, prototypicality is largely a function of ingroup/out-group relations. Members of my own group are, for me, more proto-typically human than members of any other group. As a result, I am more likely to invoke the schema "human"—including the subschema of human subjectivity—for a member of my own group, and I am more likely to invoke a more specific schema for members of another group. White peo-ple, for instance, are likely to activate the schema "human" for other white people, but to activate the schema "black" for black people (much as they would activate the more general schema for prototypical birds, but the more specific schema for eagles or vultures).

The situation is, in some ways, even more extreme than this indicates. First of all, divisions between ingroups and outgroups are always hier-archical, and not only in prototypicality. As Duckitt (1992) points out, "Ingroup members are rated more favorably than outgroup members on evaluative trait ratings" (69). An ingroup/outgroup division, moreover, is evaluative even when it has no distinct social function, even when the division is completely random. Lawrence Hirschfeld (1996) explains that "simply telling subjects that they have been assigned to certain groups is sufficient to trigger ingroup favoritism. This is no less true when people are aware that the basis for group assignment is arbitrary" (1). When people are divided into groups in an explicitly arbitrary manner (say, by whether a particular digit in their social security number is odd or even) and do not interact with one another in any way, they still judge the ac-tivities and personality traits of ingroup members more favorably than those of outgroup members (Duckitt 1992, 68–69).

The situation only worsens when one goes beyond this minimal sce-nario. "The more salient the intergroup categorization is made," notes Duckitt, "the stronger the tendency to show bias and discrimination in favor of the ingroup" (69). Plainly, then, this sort of division will be all the more consequential when it is defined in relation to such highly salient, stable, and socially functional properties as race or sex. As Hirschfeld (1996) puts it, ingroup/outgroup differences "stand out . . . to the extent that their physical correlates are clearly marked" and "that significant economic, social, and other structural consequences are associated with them" (24).

But even this is not all there is to the consensual effects of ingroup/outgroup divisions. Following Elizabeth Anscombe (1981), one may divide enjoyment into two categories: "enjoyment of substance" and "enjoyment of facts." One enjoys a substance when one enjoys the thing itself—an object or activity. One enjoys a fact when one enjoys the truth of some statement pertaining to the thing. If Jones does not care for exercise, he or she may enjoy the fact of having run three miles, but have found the experience itself (the substance) miserable. As this illustrates, the same division may be drawn for displeasure. Thus, Jones may have enjoyed the substance of sleeping all day, but may deplore the fact that he or she did this.

One might say that pleasures of substance are, for the most part, singular. They concern only themselves. The enjoyment of a substance involves an absorption in the experience of that substance—whether it is a matter of sexual pleasure, taste, or anything else. Many, perhaps all, pleasures of fact are not singular but comparative in at least three ways: with ideals, with oneself, and with others. Suppose I run three miles in twenty-four minutes. I may be pleased (take pleasure in the fact) because I had established an eight-minute mile as a sort of aspiration (comparison with an ideal). Or I may be pleased with this because it is faster than I have previously run three miles (comparison with self). Or I may be disappointed because the colleague with whom I was running completed three miles in twenty-two minutes (comparison with others).

Of these, comparison with others is typically the earliest—it is by comparison with others that one is able to evaluate oneself from childhood on. It is by comparison with others that ideals are established. In this way, the most fundamental evaluation of oneself, and thus the most fundamental pleasures in facts, derive from the comparison of oneself with others. This does not necessarily have to be crudely competitive or antagonistic. It is, in the first place, simply a necessary way of moving outside one's own narrow experience of oneself in order to understand and evaluate one's actions. To take a simple example: how am I to know whether I am running well if I have no idea how long or how fast other people run?

On the other hand, this sort of comparative evaluation tends to become crudely competitive and antagonistic if it is not transformed into an ideal, if it remains a matter of direct interpersonal comparison. Here, a further distinction might be made between comparison that forms the immediate basis for self-evaluation and comparison that serves to establish an ideal. Suppose that I have been running three miles in thirty minutes, and I find that a colleague of roughly the same age and background is running three miles in twenty-five minutes. I may compare myself directly with him or her, then feel sad and inferior, or angry and resentful. In consequence, I may set out to beat him or her, to do better than he or she does. Alternatively, I may set this up as a new ideal for myself, evaluating my future runs in terms of progress toward this goal. If I evaluate myself by direct comparison only, then I will feel good if my colleague slows down, due to some physical ailment or decline in discipline. I will be happy to the extent that the difference between us diminishes, even if I myself am running at the same pace as before. In direct comparison, then, it is relative performance or value alone that matters. It is not the absolute value of how fast I can run but the relative value of the difference between my speed and that of my colleague. As such, any harm to him or her is a good for me. This is not true when I am evaluating myself relative to an ideal.

Unfortunately, the enjoyment of facts concerning ingroup/outgroup divisions appears to be a matter of direct comparison—hence hostile, antagonistic competition—in almost every case. As already noted, "when . . . subjects are asked to allocate rewards (or punishments) between ingroup and outgroup members, they do so in a manner that maximizes the differential between ingroup and outgroup even though this may reduce the absolute benefits to the experimental subjects or even to the ingroup" (Duckitt 1992, 68–69). Moreover, if subjects are divided into ingroups and outgroups and "are given the opportunity to discriminate," they "show increased self-esteem" (85).

It is difficult to say just why this happens. It may simply be a spontaneous tendency, a basic "will to power." Perhaps people's immediate impulse is to denigrate members of any outgroup and evaluate themselves on the basis of that denigration. On the other hand, this behavior is not only cruel but so pathetic that it is hard to imagine it arising naturally out of biological development. Rather, it might be that people rely on direct comparison with others when they feel entirely unable to pursue ideals. While some people have the self-confidence and social opportunities to work to achieve ideals, others do not. Many people do not feel that the concrete conditions of their lives allow them to work toward anything other than mere survival. Living for a long time without the possibility of pursuing ideals—working overtime simply to make ends meet; trying to keep some shred of emotional health after abuse at school, home, or work—habituates one to thinking and living in the more immediate terms of direct comparison. It is not that the establishment of ideals is a luxury. It is more like a necessity, in fact. Nonetheless, it is a necessity that requires time and means, and a reservoir of self-esteem to sustain one while pursuing these ideals. Since so many people do not have the time or means, or the requisite self-confidence, it is a necessity they have learned to live without. Yet its loss continues to degrade their emotional health, reducing them to this self-harming pettiness.

In any case, whether essentialism and narcissistic/oppositional identification are the result of a natural impulse driving people to build their self-esteem on the denigration of others, or the conditions of inequality that inhibit the formation and pursuit of ideals, or some other factor, it is at least clear that such identification and self-evaluation can be fostered or inhibited by society. Moreover, it is apparent that currently they are not inhibited but fostered, both as a series of specific identifications and a general mode of thought. For example, the family, education, newsmedia, and entertainment industry all contribute to the creation of an essentializing and oppositional gender identity. The family is structured along gender lines, and the child is understood in gender terms from birth, through all the stereotyped rituals of family behavior—from dressing male and female children differently to playing with or even speaking to them differently (see Gleason 1987; see also Fausto-Sterling 1985, 36). These differences are marked in oppositional terms as well, with actions and objects that are "for boys" being sharply distinguished from those that are "for girls."

Spectator sports provide a striking portrait of a social practice that encourages narcissistic and oppositional thinking in more general and obviously competitive ways. The point of school or team spirit is to "support" the home side—to cheer it on, rejoice in its victories, and take pride in its accomplishments, while vilifying and loathing the opponent. In other words, the point is to identify narcissistically with the team in an oppositional manner, and base at least a part of one's self-esteem on the superiority or inferiority of the home team relative to its rivals. This is true not only in professional sports but perhaps even more significantly in school sports, especially high school sports with their often long-standing rivalries and associated rituals, from "pep rallies" to elaborate "homecoming" celebrations.

In this context, it is not surprising that sporting metaphors, and even direct connections with sporting events, were so common in the discussion and celebration of the Gulf War. The manufacture of consent for the war was intimately bound up with the narcissistic and oppositional principles of sport, from the widespread insistence that all Americans must "support the troops"—an insistence that the troops be cheered to victory like a sports team—to the flag waving at the Super Bowl and the *Victory in the Desert* video produced by NFL films (see "Victory" 1991, 63), from General Norman Schwartzkopf's use of football plays to explain military strategy and Bush's naming the war his "Super Bowl" (64), to one infantryman's boast about killing twenty-seven Iraqi soldiers, "It seemed like high school, going into a football game. We were hyped up" (Colhoun 1991, 4; see also Andersen 1991, 4). As Salman Rushdie (1989) remarks in *Shame*, a good commander understands "the intimate relationship between sport and war" (221).

But the oppositional function of sport is not confined to war, or to the generalized reinforcement of competitive narcissism. Ian Buruma (1992) reports an experience that illustrates how it can operate to strengthen quite specific identifications and oppositions: "A week before Christmas I went to see a soccer match between teams from Rotterdam and Amsterdam, once a city with many Jews. I had the misfortune to sit with the Rotterdam supporters, about 20,000 of them, who bellowed 'Jewish dogs' every time an Amsterdam player had the ball. When the Amsterdam player happened to be black, he was a 'Jewish nigger' " (16).

Up to this point, the focus has been on more or less straightforward cases of identification with members of an ingroup. There are instances, however, in which oppressed people do not identify with members of their own group but with those of the dominant group. This should briefly be considered before moving on, for it has significant ramifications for fostering consent.

"Cross identification," as one might call it, has been most directly and widely attested among black children (see Hirschfeld 1996, 138). Specifically, many black children, when faced with pictures of black and white youth, explicitly identify themselves with the image of a white child, rather than that of a black one. This sort of thing is no doubt found among adults as well—if necessarily in a less naive form, a form that includes a sense that such cross identification is not only mistaken but socially impossible. Take the character Eliza in Peter Abrahams's (1989) *Mine Boy*, who declares, "Inside I am not black and I do not want to be a black person" (60).

What appears to be going on here is that the prototype human for these particular black people is white, and they are simply associating themselves with that image. While that seems innocuous enough in and of itself, the effects of this "reverse prototypicality" on solidarity among the oppressed should be immediately obvious. The effects on an individual's emotional stability and sense of self-worth may be less apparent, but equally serious. Abrahams vividly portrays Eliza's mood swings, vacillations in self-esteem, and erratic behavior, as she shifts back and forth in her conception of herself and her understanding of what constitutes a prototypical human.

In some ways a more extreme form of this same sort of cross-identification may be found in such pathological phenomena as what psychoanalysts call "identification with the aggressor" (see Freud 1966, chapter 9). Oppression involves humiliation and physical suffering. If the suffering or humiliation is intense and prolonged enough, it gives rise to trauma. People are traumatized when they cannot rid themselves of the obsessive and painful recollection of the past, or a correlated fear of the future, when their lives come to be structured around trying to rid themselves of the memories and nightmares, or trying to avoid the return of the misery. In more pathological cases, individuals may, unconsciously, try to change that trauma, as if they could travel back in time and relive the moment.

There are two ways in which someone might try, unconsciously, pathologically, to remake a traumatic past. As just noted, they might take up the position of the person who inflicted the suffering. If Smith was traumatized by a beating as a child, he or she might relive and simultaneously repudiate the trauma by becoming a child beater him- or herself. Conversely, one might try to seduce one's torturer, inspire his or her love, like a wife who responds to her husband's beatings with still more kindness in the hope of drawing love out of his hate.

Suppose now that the traumatic suffering was not merely personal, but based on some narcissistic opposition, such as race. Racism clearly can produce deep traumas, when, for example, white faculty in a university setting continually harass and demean a nonwhite colleague, insulting him or her at every opportunity, derogating his or her work, accusing him or her of criminal behavior without evidence of any kind. There are many ways that one can respond to this sort of treatment. One might join in deeper and more thorough solidarity with other people who are subjected to the same treatment, working toward a more decent society for all. But one does not always have a choice about these things, and sometimes the trauma is so emotionally destructive that it produces pathological forms of behavior. One receives what psychoanalysts refer to as a "narcissistic wound," a devastation of one's self-esteem, and one tries to heal it by repudiating the entire scenario. In one version, one might identify with the aggressor, behaving in the same cruel way to other minorities, making them suffer precisely the same trauma. In another, one becomes the emotional slave of white people, organizing one's whole life around a quest for their approval and affection, as if that will soothe and close up the sore left by their earlier cruelty.

The same thing happens with women and sexism. Traumatized in her own tenure review, due to the misogyny of her colleagues, Jones may join in genuine solidarity with other women—and minorities and others who suffer discrimination—to work against unjust treatment. Yet she might equally impose the same sort of torture on women considered for tenure after her. Or she might devote the rest of her career to earning the respect of men in her department, gearing her work to produce just that effect.

In short, some pain may provoke resistance. But great pain is as likely to arouse pathological and debilitating varieties of consent—indeed, not merely consent but positive devotion to the system of cruelty that caused the pain to begin with.

COGNITIVE EXEMPLA

This discussion of trauma and identification with the aggressor leads to the topic of transference: a particular, pathological form of thought and action based on "exempla." Before going on to transference, however, more ordinary forms of exemplum-based cognition and behavior need to be considered.

Understanding anyone involves a complex of memories, feelings, generalizations, and expectations, built up from one's experience of the person in question as well as experiences of and common beliefs about persons identified as members of the same group. If I hear that Jones is interested in postmodernism, I have certain beliefs, expectations, and feelings regarding him or her even before we meet. Some of these are schematic or prototypical. Yet some may be derived from particular postmodernists I have known; some may be based not on generalizations (that is, schemas and prototypes) but on specific instances. Indeed, when an object (such as another person) triggers an exemplum, so that the exemplum becomes particularly salient, it will most often override conceptualization in terms of schemas or prototypes.

This is well attested in psychological research. Richard E. Nisbett and Lee Ross (1980) illustrate the final point by a story about a bad Volvo (15; I have altered their example slightly). Suppose Smith has decided to buy a car. He reads all the relevant consumer reports and forms schemas for various types of cars. His schema for "Volvo" includes all the statistical properties he has read about, such as very high reliability. Smith has already decided that his major concern in choosing a new car is reliability. This should make Volvo one of his top choices. His brother-in-law, however, owned a Volvo that had an endless series of mechanical problems. Smith knows perfectly well that this single instance has no real implications regarding a Volvo he himself might purchase. A Volvo is still the most likely to be reliable, whatever problems his brother-in-law may have had. Nonetheless, he decides not to buy a Volvo—precisely because the salient exemplum has overriden the encompassing schema.

Exempla can operate to foster consent in a variety of ways. Indeed, they are particularly effective ideologically, for the same reason that they frequently override schemas: they are often highly salient and affectively charged. They are much more noticeable and much more likely to provoke some strong emotion—joy, anger, or fear. When I was a college student, the Bakke case certainly stood for many people as definitive of the consequences of affirmative action. At roughly the same time, Khomeini stood as a definitive exemplum of Islam for a broad range of people in the United States. Exempla may also be nameless, ordinary. For instance, whenever one conceives of or responds to current situations by reference to an anecdote, one is cognitively guided by an exemplum. In his studies of racist discourse, Teun van Dijk (1987) has found that racist anecdotes—concerning a friend who was mugged by a black man, a black woman who was trying to cheat a grocer, and so on—are a particularly common and effective way of communicating racism. In fact, racist speech shows a particularly high reliance on exempla (157).

Ronald Reagan's tales about welfare queens fall into the same category—except that they were communicated nationwide, from a national authority, not told by an ordinary person in private conversation. As such, Reagan's anecdotes no doubt helped to consolidate the antagonism toward welfare that resulted in the cruel reform passed under Clinton. Again, exempla are salient and emotive, and thus, are likely to have far more motivational force than any schema formed out of statistical analysis. A bloodless statistic about the number of children who will be undernourished due to welfare reform is likely to be superseded in motivational force by a vivid story about a fat black woman driving around in her Cadillac to collect a dozen welfare checks. Indeed, the anecdote is likely to carry greater weight in subjective estimates of probability. As Norbert Schwarz (1995) has pointed out, drawing on extensive psychological research, "We estimate the frequency, likelihood, or typicality of an event by the ease with which we can bring relevant examples to mind" (371)—in other words, people estimate general patterns less by reference to schemas embodying those patterns than by salient exempla.

Of course, this is not to say that exempla preclude schemas. They tend instead to generate their own schemas; in other words, salient exempla tend to foster the formation of schemas, even if these are contradicted by statistics (compare van Dijk 1987, 198). Moreover, standard schemas, common stereotypes (usually a form of prototype), and salient exempla tend to reinforce one another—again, independent of statistical plausibility. As a consequence of this mutual reinforcement, "stories about ethnic minority groups are easier to find [that is, they are more cognitively salient, more prone to cognitive access] when they feature instantiations of stereotypical prejudices" (ibid., 279).

Recall, for example, the way in which George Bush's presidential campaign used William Horton's escape on furlough, and his subsequent crime, to defame Michael Dukakis's "liberal" policies as governor of Massachusetts—a straightforward use of a salient exemplum toward ideological ends. Clearly, a single case of this sort has no implications whatsoever for an understanding of Dukakis's policies—even his furlough program. Indeed, statistically, the furlough program operated to *reduce* the number of crimes overall. David Anderson (1995) observes that in "comparing those who had gone out on furloughs and participated in other pre-release programs with those who had not, they found that the programs substantially and consistently contributed to reduced recidivism." As such, "ending furloughs would likely result in a net *increase* in crime" (109). This does not matter, however. The image/exemplum of (black) Horton raping a defenseless (white) woman was highly salient, memorable, and emotive—inspiring a sort of terror in anyone who might identify with his victim or her friends and relatives. It was, of course, far more salient and emotive than the schematic, statistically supported abstractions cited by Dukakis in defense of his program.

This exemplum could be used easily for ideological purposes because of its coherence with ideologically functional schemas, such as the standard racist one of black men as rapists. Indeed, the case was systematically misrepresented in such a way as to conform to such schemas. For instance, one distortion concerned Horton's earlier crime, which was falsely presented as cannibalistic (Anderson 1995, 184)—drawing on the old colonial stereotypes about Africans.

Another important schema did not concern Horton but Dukakis—the schema of "liberals" as excessively lenient toward, and overly sympathetic with, criminals. This schema functions ideologically to establish Democratic Party crime policies as the "far Left" of the spectrum of rational opinion. If Democrats can be characterized as too lenient, then anything to their left must be irrational. Note that this is an ideological claim in which the Democrats are likely to be complicit, for they do not want any competitor to their left, and thus, have every motive to assist in characterizing liberal Democrats as the reasonable extreme of the political spectrum.

Perhaps most interestingly, the entire case fit a sort of narrative schema of random, violent crime, isolated by Anderson (1995) as particularly important in the United States over the preceding decade. This schema has five basic components: the crimes are "luridly violent"; the victims are "middle-class, usually white" and the perpetrators usually black; the victims are innocent; the victims were chosen at random; and the criminals had "some history of involvement with the criminal justice system, suggesting that if the system had only worked better, the terrible crime might have been avoided" (5–6). When one examines the way in which the Horton case was presented, it is clear that it was widely viewed through this schema—with relevant aspects highlighted and others downplayed, with elements filled in according to this pregiven structure, etc. Anderson points out that the schema had such force that white criminals, such as Charles Stuart and Susan Smith, used a version of it to cover up their own crimes, blaming these crimes on black assailants (7–8; these were not isolated instances—for a series of related cases, see Russell 1998, chapter 5). Nonetheless, it is the exemplum that has the emotive and motivational force, not the schema alone.

I have been speaking thus far as if the exempla in question were at least putatively true. Exempla, however, can be explicitly fictional without losing their potential cognitive force. Television programs, movies, novels, and plays all provide people with exempla through which they think and feel about the world. This is one reason why the portrayal of, say, blacks or Arabs in these media is so politically important. Any prominent minority character from television to cinema can be taken up and operate as an exemplum. Indeed, this is why it is important to have a wide range of black, Arab, gay, lesbian, and other characters, so that none is likely to have the unique salience necessary to operate as an exemplum. For even a positive exemplum is, in these cases, problematic. A single exemplum of, say, gay men still conduces toward the view that gay men form a single, homogenous group.

It should be stressed that I am not saying people are too stupid to know the difference between fact and fiction. The point is, rather, that everyone's cognitive apparatus is structured in such a way that a vivid image is likely to have significant motivational effects, even when it is fictional—even when people recognize that it is fictional. My guess is that fiction is, on the whole, more effective than truth or putative truth when it comes to providing exempla of broader categories, such as war. People's experience of real war is always limited and fragmentary. But the experience of fictional war, most obviously on film, has a fullness, structure, and necessity. Star Wars or Independence Day provides a "complete" sense of a war—its background, motives, progress, and resolution. Films depict human stories of the "good guys" in detail, fostering identification; they show the perfidy of the "bad guys." For these reasons, it seems likely that these fictional wars are, for most people, more salient and emotive, and hence more likely to stand as motivationally consequential cognitive exempla, than real wars. When Star Wars first came out, it seemed immediately obvious that its division into the good rebels and religious-mystical Jedi, on the one hand, and the evil empire, on the other, would operate for ordinary people as an exemplum for conceiving of and responding to the United States and Soviet Union. Ronald Reagan made use of this parallel in referring to the USSR as the "evil empire," and even more so in propagandizing for his Strategic Defense Initiative (SDI), nicknamed, of course, "Star Wars."

Note that in keeping with this, exempla do not, for the most part, operate consciously. They are typically not objects of self-reflective scrutiny, and thus, are akin to motivational rather than self-conscious beliefs. Indeed, the vast majority of inferences, conceptualizations, and the like proceed unconsciously, whether they are based on exempla, prototypes, or schemas. That is one of the primary reasons why they can be so effective in these cases. A self-conscious comparison of Reagan's SDI with George Lucas's film may have some motivational force. But the real effect of linking the two in people's minds derives from the unconscious transferral of identification, feeling, and so forth. Suppose people identify strongly with the heroes of *Star Wars* whose lives are saved by the use of laser weapons; suppose filmgoers feel fear for them when facing the evil empire, then rejoice with them when they triumph using these weapons; suppose viewers feel a mild, vicarious lift in their self-esteem as the fair-haired and light-skinned heroes with whom they identify triumph over the swarthy out-group of evil—all of which I take to be a pretty standard response to the movie. People are unlikely to draw any self-conscious conclusions about SDI based on these feelings. Once SDI has been linked with these feelings, however, people are far more likely to support it. This is due to the non-conscious, motivational force of salient and emotive exempla. The situation here is parallel to that of Nisbett and Ross's Volvo. Even a mass of technical analysis from reliable physicists and engineers is unlikely to overcome an enthusiasm for SDI that is derived from its link with *Star Wars*, just as a mass of consumer reports is unlikely to overcome Smith's aversion to Volvos, derived from the case of his brother-in-law.

Even if a person does decide to go against the exemplum and oppose SDI, it is quite possible that the exemplum will dull this opposition, so that he or she will be less likely to take concrete steps to prevent its implementation. It may, in other words, reduce his or her opposition to "prompted assent" (or "prompted dissent")—a belief that not only lacks motivational force but is not even maintained self-consciously and continuously, a belief that arises only when prompted by a question (as in, for example, an opinion poll).

Of course, exempla are not in and of themselves consensual. They are no more intrinsically ideological than beliefs. This is what makes left-wing, feminist, and antiracist literature and cinema so important. Still, exemplum-based thought can be exploited to consensual ends with ease. This is particularly evident in majority/minority relations. Simply due to the nature of salience—it is, in part, a function of rarity—the reduction of minorities to exempla will necessarily be far more widespread than that of majorities to exempla (see, for instance, Nisbett and Ross 1980, 239). This is problematic, because negative characteristics or events are likely to be more salient and carry greater emotional force than positive ones. For example, a crime will always have greater salience than ordinary noncriminal action, or even an unusual act of benevolence, whoever is involved. Therefore, criminal and other "deviant" acts by members of minority groups will be particularly salient and likely to be taken as exemplary. If one black man commits robbery and another makes a large donation to charity, these will not cancel one another out in their psychological effects and ideological consequences.

More generally, differences in salience are part of the reason members of a minority group are evaluated more negatively, even when the characteristics that define them as a minority are perceived as neutral. This has been demonstrated in research by David Hamilton and R. K. Gifford. Test subjects were shown sentences describing members of two groups, "A" and "B." Group A was twice the size of Group B, but otherwise the groups were *identical.* In keeping with this, members of the two groups engaged in "undesirable behaviors" at exactly the same rate. Nevertheless, test subjects consistently overestimated the undesirable behaviors of members of the smaller group, rated that group less favorably, and so on (see Hamilton and Trolier 1986, 136). The situation is only going to be worse when there are preexisting stereotypes about the groups (such as when the groups are distinguished racially), stereotypes that further distort experience and memory through confirmatory bias.

TRANSFERENCE

Up to this point, the use of exempla has been explored in relation to persons or events of the same, politically consequential category—exempla of blacks guiding people's thought about and action toward other blacks, exempla drawn from one war (perhaps a fictional one) guiding feeling and response to other (real) wars. Yet there is another way in which exempla are politically consequential. There are certain occasions on which exempla are applied across putatively definitive or essential categories. For the most part, such cross-categorical connections are, so to speak, ad hoc and have little enduring consequence. Jones meets one particular Muslim, Akbar. Akbar happens to wear the same type of unusual glasses worn by Jones's close friend, Smith. This link happens to trigger the exemplum of Smith in Jones's mind, making him feel quite friendly toward Akbar, despite his general ill will toward Muslims—and despite the fact that Jones does not in general respond (self-consciously or motivationally) to "type of eyewear" as an interpretively or evaluatively relevant category. This sort of thing is common. But it is also unsystematic, and it is therefore politically inconsequential in most cases.

There is one particular case of this general sort that is systematic, however: transference. That is, the unconscious and partially pathological guidance of thought, feeling, and action by (unconscious) infantile exempla—primarily drawn from early fantasies concerning parents. The most psychologically consequential exempla are the first: the deeply ambivalent, oedipal exempla of one's parents—imagoes, as psychoanalysts call them. These imagoes remain with people from childhood, unconscious and deeply involved with repressed fantasies about other people and about themselves. In these fantasies, the imagoes are, as psychoanalysts say, "split," divided into multiple versions so that one may speak of distinct types of maternal imago, paternal imago, or even self-imago.

Any exemplum is, of course, an idea of a thing, not the thing itself. Jones's exemplum of Khomeini is not Khomeini himself but a conception of Khomeini, a conception that is not only necessarily incomplete but may be wildly inaccurate. Indeed, there are exempla that do not correspond to any real person at all, as in the case of fictional characters. Similarly, there may be two entirely different exempla of one person. Suppose Jones has heard things about "the Ayatollah" and "Khomeini." He forms ideas about both, and uses both as exempla, without ever realizing that they are the same person. Fantasies present an even more elaborated form of just this division between exemplum and reality. Suppose Jones is infatuated with Smith. In real life, Smith treats Jones badly. But in Jones's fantasy life, Smith is warmly affectionate. There is a sense in which it could be said that Jones's idea of Smith had been "split" into the unfriendly, real Smith, and the affectionate, imaginary one. This can even happen independent of fantasy. Suppose I can't quite figure Jones out. One minute, I think he or she is being friendly, but the next minute I find him or her insulting. So I form two different conceptions of Jones. In one, Jones is convivial, friendly, and the seeming insults are intended as good-natured ribbing. In the other, Jones is hostile, and the seeming friendliness is just a strategy to prevent reprisals. Here, too, one might say that I have "split" my conception of Jones.

In psychoanalytic theory, the same sort of thing occurs with infantile imagoes. However, these are far more important than any other exempla. Indeed, these infantile imagoes, as one's first instances of persons, are equally one's founding instances of persons, the basic exempla on which all subsequent exempla are to some degree based. Due to his or her ambivalent, conflicted, confusing relations with all-powerful parents, the child too splits his or her parental imagoes. In general terms, this split may be characterized as one between affectionate and antagonistic. But there are many possible subdivisions within each category. According to classical psychoanalysis, the most common splits of the paternal imago would include the protecting father, the "castrated" or powerless father, and the "castrating" or aggressively hostile father. The most common splits of the maternal imago would include the nurturant mother, the withdrawn or inaccessible mother, and the devouring mother (who subsumes the child's whole being in her own).

Transference is, roughly, the unconscious incorporation of one or another parental imago into one's understanding of, affective response to, and behavior toward some person in one's contemporary environment. It is the use of an infantile imago as an exemplum, but it goes beyond this as well, for it simultaneously involves the unconscious incorporation of the "target" or contemporary person into a set of repressed infantile fantasies, and a sort of indirect enactment of those fantasies. When the transference includes the idealizing and affectionate elements of these imagoes, it is referred to as "positive"; when it incorporates the degraded or threatening elements, it is referred to as "negative." Both sorts of transference can play a significant role in fostering consent.

It is no doubt immediately evident when one reads of the most common forms of splitting that the fantasies surrounding parental imagoes are by no means simply natural or spontaneous. To a great extent, the oedipal fantasies of a child are the product of a particular social structure, one in which women are in charge of immediate child care (hence nurturance) while men are given primary responsibility over the family's relation to the world at large (hence protection). Thus, a typical idealized father imago establishes the father, and anyone onto whom this imago is transferred, as an absolute source of knowledge, power, and protection. One typical idealized mother imago establishes the mother as sexually pure and selflessly nurturant. These imagoes mirror a patriarchal structure, associating men with intellect and domination or aggressive action, and women with bodily care and service.

Clearly, such imagoes not only derive from patriarchal structures, they contribute to the preservation of such structures as well. When manifest in ethical discussions, political actions, or social behaviors, they repeat and thus reinforce the patriarchal relations that gave rise to them initially. Movies and television shows, news programs, and magazine articles, moreover, all tacitly invoke these imagoes by, for example, contrasting the heartless businesswoman with the affectionate wife and mother—a recurrent structure in recent television and cinema, as Susan Faludi (1991) has stressed. In doing this, they not only foster consciously conformist beliefs and attitudes (say, those that condemn highly independent women) but also link these with powerful unconscious imagoes: the devouring mother and the nurturant mother, in this case. (Note that it is immaterial whether or not writers, directors, and producers are thinking in psychoanalytic terms when creating such works. All they need recognize is that a certain sort of opposition is particularly emotionally effective. Psychoanalytic theory may be necessary to explain why it is so effective, but no one needs psychoanalytic theory to see that it is effective, and thus to produce it.)

The activation of imagoes in these and other ways is consequential, for transference motivates, excites, and angers. People hold many beliefs about which they are relatively indifferent. There is no reason that this should not be the case with respect to some unscrupulous businesswomen and some loving wives out in the general populace or on television. Part of the reason people react to these characters is a matter of self-interest; part is a matter of narcissistic identification. A large part of the reason, though, is that people's maternal imagoes still carry with them deep, infantile, conflicted, irrational feelings of love and anger, satisfaction and frustration, and these unresolved feelings—along with related beliefs, identifications, and so on—enter into one's understanding of and response to the position of women and men in society, the sexual division of labor, and the like.

Transference relations have great relevance outside gender relations as well. For example, infantile imagoes played a significant role in the Gulf War. Through a range of outlets, the imago of the absolutely knowing, powerful, protecting father was associated with the U.S. government broadly, and at a certain point linked with Norman Schwartzkopf in particular, for whom many people evidenced a classic case of transference love. This was implicit in much of the war coverage, from the unquestioning attitude of the media concerning government pronouncements to their childlike wonder at smart bombs and patriot missiles.

In other contexts, rulers have sought to associate dominant figures with paternal or, less frequently, maternal imagoes. Walter Rodney (1972) reports an unusually explicit case of this: "As late as 1949, a Principal Education Officer in Tanganyika carefully outlined that the Africans of that colony should be bombarded in primary school with propaganda about the British royal family. 'The theme of the king as father should be stressed throughout the syllabus and mentioned in every lesson,' he said" (247). This was probably too overt and crude to have actually encouraged a transference, but the relation of the two is clear enough.

Indeed, this attitude of reverence for parental, usually paternal, authority is one of the most pervasive and debilitating effects of transference in politics. As I described it above, transference appeared to have no history, but to be a direct movement from infantile experiences to some current situation. That is not true. Each transference may recontextualize and reorient the original imago in such a way as to alter subsequent transferences. The child's idealized father imago derives from the social structure of the family. Early transferences involving this imago occur in school with teachers, in church with pastors, and in other hierarchical institutional settings. Repeated transferences of this sort encourage an association of the idealized father imago with individuals who have institutional authority, or even with institutional authority as such. This may operate not only to promote consensual beliefs about particular events or situations, such as the Gulf War, but also to encourage a more general trust in the authority of dominant groups, and thus, in the social structure as a whole. Moreover, due to the traumatic impotence of children when faced with parental rage, transference may also, and simultaneously, foster an irrational fear of annihilating punishment for any form of nonconformity, exacerbating already strong tendencies in this regard.

A perhaps more obvious function of transference in the Gulf War was the negative transference onto Iraqis, and Saddam Hussein in particular. Hussein was not only dehumanized; he was repeatedly characterized in terms that encouraged an identification of him with the negative paternal imago of a violent brute and lascivious rapist—an imago already central to both antiblack and anti-Arab racism. In fact, he was implicitly characterized as a rapist of children, a particularly effective cue for the threatening oedipal imago. Some striking instances of this may be found in Bush's speech announcing the beginning of the war. (I am grateful to Marianne Sadowski for pointing this out.) Bush (1991) begins by characterizing Kuwait as a child, "small" and "helpless," that has been "crushed" and "brutalized." He goes on to contrast the "family of nations"—the phrase serves to trigger positive infantile associations—with Hussein's treatment of "tiny" (again, childlike) Kuwait, which "Saddam Hussein systematically raped." Bush further specifies Hussein's crimes as "unspeakable atrocities" against "innocent children"—an especially effective image, in context, if also one that is particularly obscene in its hypocrisy (recall the hundreds of thousands of innocent children killed because of the war and subsequent embargo [see, for example, Crossette 1995]).

More generally, the ingroup/outgroup division almost immediately draws positive transference to the hierarchical authorities of the former, and a negative transference to any prominent member of the latter—or in some cases, to any member of the latter whatsoever. Indeed, negative transference has long been seen as a primary element within racism, one of the most socially consequential forms of ingroup/outgroup division. The stereotype of the black man as absurdly sexually powerful and/or a rapist certainly fits well with the standard imago of the "phallic" father. The stereotype of the black woman as a prostitute aligns with one standard maternal imago as well—one maternal imago that would frequently be paired with the phallic father.

The transference need not stop at this rather generic level, though; it can become fully individual, too. In other words, racial stereotypes that trigger infantile imagoes may do more than yield broadly racist ideas and feelings. One's concrete relations with members of different racial groups may become deeply bound up with one's own, idiosyncratic unconscious fantasies and psychoneurotic behaviors. Though still based on typological links of the sort just mentioned, this more fully individuated form of transference—which is to say, transference proper—takes up and particularizes these typological links according to unique, personal, infantile experience and fantasy.

Doris Lessing's (1976) *The Grass Is Singing* presents a useful illustration. In this novel, Mary, the protagonist, has an especially hateful relation to blacks. She constantly abuses her domestic servants, and at one point, whips one of the farmhands for what could at worst be considered a minor impoliteness when asking for a drink (134–35). Lessing implicitly explains this as a negative transference. Specifically, she unfolds Mary's hatred for her father, while continually drawing implicit parallels between Mary's relation to her father and the black servants. For example, Mary is disturbed by "the hot acrid scent of native bodies" (187); she "shudder[ed], as . . . she imagined that native smell" (188). Lessing makes it clear that this disgust—which focuses on a racist commonplace about African odor—has oedipal roots. It derives from Mary's father's disagreeable habit of pressing Mary's head into his lap and holding her face against his crotch: "She smelled the sickly odor of beer and through it she smelled too—her head held down in the thick stuff of his trousers—the unwashed masculine smell she always associated with him. She struggled to get her head free, for she was half-suffocating, and her father held it down, laughing at her panic" (190). Mary's wild and brutal reaction to the farmhand's request for a drink is similarly explained: Mary's greatest resentment against her father concerned precisely his drinking when he should have been working. In both cases, her transferential reaction to Africans is a specification of the typological link between blacks and the lascivious rapist imago—a link signaled by the society in which she grew up ("She was afraid of them, of course. Every woman in South Africa is brought up to be" [61]). But in each instance, this typological link has been developed—in Mary's imagination and in her transferential behavior—through specific oedipal fantasies and memories from her childhood.

Needless to say, such transferential connections are not confined to literature but extend through ordinary life, from personal interactions, to dreams and fantasies, to the onset and elaboration of neuroses and psychoses. The most famous treatments of the psychopathology of race relations are to be found in the writings of Frantz Fanon. For example, Fanon (1967) discusses the case of Mlle. B., who suffered from psychoneurotic "agitation, motor instability, tics, and spasms" (204), traceable to an unconscious "fear of imaginary Negroes" (208). A recent case, reported by Katheryn Russell (1998), is in some ways even more striking, for it illustrates a sort of hysterical delusion that is both fully individuated and yet also collective. In 1994, "a White Louisiana woman told police" that she had been raped by a black man with "a tattoo of a serpent on his arm"—a classic displacement of phallic potency through the image of the snake, combined with Satanic suggestions drawn from religious myth. What is striking about this case is that the woman "confessed that she had made up the rape story." Nonetheless, when a police sketch was circulated in Baton Rouge, "twenty-eight other women notified the police that they too had been assaulted by the imaginary 'serpent man' " (77). Even at its most individually psychopathological, the racialized imago is social in its operation and political in its function. In this instance, it was directly bound up with the legal system and police, and could easily have resulted in an arrest, even a conviction.

In conclusion, it is worth turning to another aspect of transference and the oedipal complex. Oedipal imagoes, as already noted, involve images of oneself just as they involve images of one's parents. These self-imagoes, too, are ambivalent and multiple. Most obviously, there is the "innocent" ego, the good boy or girl whose acts, ideas, and feelings are all just what they should be, and the "guilty" ego—the ego who desires one parent and wants to kill the other, the ego that does things that are wrong and provokes his or her parents, the ego that brings on punishment, which is to say, threats of "castration" or annihilation. Indeed, children sometimes refer to themselves by two different names, explaining that a "naughty" act was done by "bad Billy" rather than "good Billy," and sometimes even expressing the desire to be rid of their "bad" self entirely.

These imagoes can be transferred, or rather "projected," onto others as well. This can be particularly dangerous, because the repudiation of the "bad" self-imago is often extreme and bound up with other pathological relations. For example, the person who most deeply fears annihilating punishment for nonconformity may also be the most vehement in demanding the annihilation of anyone else who violates the principles of the system even slightly. Perhaps the clearest case of this is homophobia. As recent studies have demonstrated, a strong antipathy toward gay men is most often found among putatively heterosexual men who have strong homosexual impulses, but have repressed those impulses. The intensity of their malice toward gay men is a direct result of their own panic over being "bad" themselves (see Adams, Wright, and Lohr 1996). It seems apparent that the same sort of self-repudiation underlies many types of hierarchy-preserving, conformism-inducing hatred and aggression.

FOUR   Cognitive Structure and

the Example of Racism

In the preceding chapter, I introduced some complex cognitive structures—schemas, prototypes, and exempla—that go beyond a folk psychology of beliefs and aims. Though I touched on schemas and prototypes, only exempla were treated in detail. In this final chapter, prototypes in particular will be considered more thoroughly, along with two further aspects of cognition: domains and models. But before going on to this, the organization of the mental lexicon needs to be examined.

LEXICAL STRUCTURE

Perhaps the first thing I should stress is that all the cognitive structures discussed here—and thus all concepts, vocabulary items, linguistic and conceptual principles, and so forth—exist only in individual people's minds. All humans may be understood to have a sort of internal "lexicon," something like a mental dictionary/encyclopedia. This internal lexicon is largely the same from person to person within any given social and linguistic community—otherwise, those people would not be able to communicate successfully. On the other hand, there will be some variation in the extent of conceptual differentiation (some people will, for example, distinguish more types of flowers), in the precise structuring and content of particular lexical entries (individuals will give slightly different definitions even to common terms), and so on.

This lexicon may be viewed as structured into clusters of conceptual and perceptual properties and relations, usually linked with words. Thus, each person has a cluster of properties linked with the word "cat" (animal, furry, smallish, four-legged, pet, makes "meow" sound). These properties are ordered into a default hierarchy, with the most important properties listed at the "top." Top-to-bottom order here refers not to a spatial arrangement but rather to definitional importance and order of access in cognition: "animal" is more essential than "furry"; "furry" is more crucial than "pet," and so on. If a particular thing is not an animal but a vegetable, people know for certain that it is not a cat; if it is bald, people are likely to doubt that it is a cat, but they will not be certain from that fact alone; if it is not a pet, people are unlikely to see this as providing a good reason for doubting its catness.

On the other hand, if it is not a pet, it is likely to be seen as a less proto-typical cat. As noted in the preceding chapter, lexical entries are not only hierarchized but also structured into defaults. The default conception of a cat includes "pet." Defaults may be overridden, often for specified alterna-tives—in this case, "stray cat" or "alley cat." The more defaults that are in place, the closer the cat in question is to a prototypical cat.

Within the default hierarchy, there appear to be several subclasses of information. Thus people probably distinguish the subcluster "common beliefs about" for any lexical entry. Common beliefs about cats would include, for example, "disloyal" and "sneaky." Such common beliefs are always candidates for inclusion in the main attributive subdirectory of the entry for the lexical item at hand. By "main attributive subdirectory," I mean the part of one's lexical entry listing properties that one implicitly attributes to cats. While I may currently have no opinion about whether or not cats are disloyal and sneaky, I may in the future see a cat behave in a certain way that leads me to conclude that this common belief is, in fact, correct. Since these common beliefs are stored in my lexical entry for cats, they are always in some degree cognitively present when I see, respond to, or think about cats. They are always open to access and inclusion in the main attributive subdirectory. They are, indeed, always available for use in understanding cats, even if I never incorporate them into the main attribu-tive subdirectory. Put differently, the structure of the human mind is such that standard, communal beliefs on any given topic (such as cats) are always readily available to me for understanding that topic, even if I do not accept those beliefs myself.

This cognitive tendency has directly consensual and conformist effects. It seems likely that everyone in the United States, whether white or black, has a category of "common beliefs about" blacks in their lexical entry for "black." This category might include, for example, "lazy." Thus, even for those who have not incorporated this property into the main attributive subdirectory of their entry (that is, even for those who do not believe that blacks are lazy), the property is always somewhere in the lexical entry, ready to be accessed and applied. This would not be a problem in and of itself were it not for the cognitive tendency toward confirmatory bias, a tendency exacerbated by the likelihood that any confirmatory instance will be more salient in this case than a disconfirmatory one. In other words, any person not doing his or her work is likely to be more salient than any number of persons doing their work—a point that does not affect whites as there is no relevant lexicalized property that might be accessed to categorize them as "lazy." As such, the mere presence of common beliefs about blacks—or Asians, gay men, or whatever—will exert a sort of ideological pressure on an understanding of and response to people and situations, even when those beliefs are repudiated. The sort of discrepancies discussed by Nisbett and Ross—where a white man on a park bench is interpreted one way and a black man another—can result even when people do not precisely hold the racist beliefs in question. The mere knowledge of a common racist belief that blacks are lazy may be enough to push a person's interpretation in that direction in any particular case.

Note that the same thing holds for, say, war, socialism, or any other ideologically consequential concern. The common belief that leftists are totalitarians (or that they fall into two categories, totalitarians and dreamy utopianists) is always open to access, and "confirmation," when one encounters a single leftist whose behavior, though perhaps merely abrasive, may be interpreted as totalitarian.

Other subdirectories of lexical structure might include "ideal" and related evaluative categories. The structure and genesis of these categories is more complex than might initially be evident. For example, as I am using the term, the "ideal" subdirectory of a lexical entry is not generated individually. Indeed, it is distinguishable from a "personal preference" subcategory. "Ideal," here, is social. Moreover, it is distinguishable not only from personal preference but also from "common preference" in society at large. The "ideal" wine, in my lexicon, may not be the wine I personally prefer or I take to be most commonly preferred in the United States but the wine preferred by a particular group, "experts."

As Hilary Putnam (1975) has stressed (in a nonpolitical context), many lexical entries involve a key reference to expertise. My entry for "quark," for example, runs something like this: "Perhaps indivisible constituent of protons, etc.; for precise meaning, consult particle physicist aware of current developments." Even "cat" includes something along the lines of "exact delimitation provided by zoologists." Ideals are regularly defined by expertise. In some instances, this is directly parallel to the descriptive cases just mentioned and a matter of scientific expertise—as in, say, the "(ideal) cholesterol level." Here, one often has no distinct categories for personal or social preference. Other instances, however, are not categorized as scientific knowledge but as taste. These too involve reference to experts, but in these cases ideal and personal preference subcategories are far more likely to diverge.

Indeed, in these cases, it makes more sense to distinguish "common preference" and "prestige" subdirectories. It could then be said that when the prestige category is assumed to be objective (most obviously, when it is assumed to rest on scientific knowledge, as in the example of cholesterol levels), then it is an ideal. As Pierre Bourdieu (1984) has argued at length, what I am calling the prestige sub-category derives largely from common preference within a social and cultural elite (much as the ideal subcategory derives largely from a scientific elite). The prestige wine is the wine preferred by that elite; the prestige music is the music preferred by that elite, and so on. Bourdieu's researches primarily concern class differences within European (specifically French) society. The point, however, applies equally to colonialist, racist, and other forms of hierarchy. In each case, the prestige category is a function of the preferences of the dominant group.

The effect of this is obvious. The cultural ideas, beliefs, and practices of the subordinated group are demeaned. The elite themselves come to be viewed as more discriminating, more insightful, etc.—circularly. Their preferences define prestige; preference for prestige items implies discrimination or "good taste"; thus their preference proves their discrimination. Note that this is true even for those who self-consciously reject the prestige standard. Much as common beliefs are always present in one's lexical entries, available for access and application, so too are prestige standards. Even if a black nationalist affirms black culture, the (repudiated) white prestige standard is always there, exerting the pressure of a social belief, reinforced by confirmatory bias.

As the last example indicates, it is not merely the origin but the content of prestige standards that is consequential. Some striking instances of particular prestige standards with consensual and conformist results may be found in beauty. Consider the image of female beauty that has been widely if tacitly disseminated by the fashion and diet industries in recent decades, and that has proven deeply important for women's self-understanding and behavior. Susan Faludi (1991) has argued powerfully that in recent years, the fashion industry, entertainment industry, and beauty and women's magazines have projected a model of feminine beauty defined by "frailty, pallor, puerility" (203). The debilitating effects of this prestige standard are not only indirect—inhibition, loss of self-esteem, etc.; they are brutally direct as well. "Antiwrinkle treatments exposed [women] to carcinogens. Acid face peels burned their skin. Silicone injections left painful deformities. 'Cosmetic' liposuction caused severe complications, infections, and even death. Internalized, the decade's beauty dictates played a role in exacerbating an epidemic of eating disorders" (ibid.). Plastic surgery drained women's resources. One survey "by a plastic surgery association found that about half their patients made less than $25,000 a year; these women took out loans and even mortgaged homes to pay the surgery bill" (218). And this is not an insignificant group of people. The number of women with breast implants alone numbers in the millions (ibid.).

Moreover, at an ideological level, advertisements and magazine articles repeatedly contrast beauty with work. Faludi cites "ad after ad" in which "the beauty industry hammered home its version of the backlash thesis: women's professional progress had downgraded their looks; equality had created worry lines and cellulite" (202). Mademoiselle, for one, warned that work can "play havoc with your complexion," lead to a "loss of hair," and result in "weight gain," especially for "high-achieving women" (ibid.).

As all this illustrates, the prestige standard of appearance affects women most obviously. Yet it also affects minorities—as is made clear by the array of hair-straightening and skin-whitening products, so widespread in the first half of the twentieth century. Indeed, the origin of rhinoplasty ("nose jobs") was racialist. It was first used to "cure" people of "Irish" pug noses and reduce the "Semitic" appearance of Jews (Gilman 1991, 184 ff.). The racialism has hardly disappeared. Faludi (1991) reports a public lecture by plastic surgeon Robert Harvey (San Francisco's "leading breast enlargement surgeon"): "The first set of slides are almost all photos of Asian women whose features he has Occidentalized—making them, in Harvey's opinion, 'more feminine' " (214).

These sorts of prestige standards plainly have debilitating, and thus consensual, effects. One might argue, however, that it is the fault of the people who accept this standard. If they rejected it, the standard would not have the same impact. This is partially true, but it ignores two essential points. The first is something I have already stressed. No one need accept a prestige standard for it to have significant consequences for their self-esteem, interactions with other people, and so forth. Its mere presence in the lexical entry has consequences in these areas. Second, the prestige standards of beauty are socially functionalized; they have real, direct outcomes for social well-being. Most obviously, they affect one's social life, and one's social life plays a crucial role not only in personal happiness but material security. In addition, they often enter directly into whether one is hired for a job or promoted once employed. This is clearly true of jobs that involve some direct focus on appearance (such as actors or spokespersons). Yet it is true elsewhere as well. Peter Passell (1994) remarks that "new studies show that men and women . . . who are rated below average in attractiveness by survey interviewers typically earn 10 to 20 percent less than those rated above average." Given the nature of the prestige standards, which are more extreme and socially valued for women than men, it is not surprising that "obese women" are perhaps the most severely affected. They "lived in households with, on average, $6,700 less in yearly income" (ibid.).

It is worth noting in this context that evaluative preferences may have consensual and conformist effects independent of elite derivation, ideological manipulation, etc. Spontaneous personal preference regarding appearance, for example, is likely to favor majorities over minorities and elites over nonelites. Simply put, other things being equal, judgments of beauty tend toward the statistical mean. The most beautiful face is the most average face (see Langlois and Roggman 1990). Distinctive features of any group, then, will have an effect on preferences relative to their number—or more exactly, to their visibility. Visibility is related to number, although it is not solely a function of it. If members of a minority group—such as white South Africans—are overrepresented in the media, then their distinctive features will have proportionately greater pull on the determination of judgments of beauty. Needless to say, the opulent few, or at least members of the same ingroups as the opulent few, tend to be the ones with disproportionately high visibility (for instance, on the overrepresentation of blond hair among women cover models and centerfolds, see Rich and Cash 1993). If blacks are a small, nonelite minority and whites are a large majority, comprising the elite, then the spontaneous preference of most people regarding skin color and beauty may be slightly darker than that of whites in general, but will certainly be far lighter than that of blacks in general. In short, it will greatly favor whites over blacks.

The situation is only worsened by the fact that any given prestige category may be linked with many other admired or ideal properties. Specifically, various types of ideals and prestige standards tend to cluster together in people's lexicons, almost to the point of mutual identification. This is probably due to their common presence in some sort of idealized prototype person. But this clustering is not confined to an idealized prototype; crucially, it spreads to real cases—real cases based at least in part on status in social hierarchies.

Consider, for example, one study in which a researcher played tapes of different Cockney and prestige-accent English voices to test subjects, then asked these subjects to grade the speakers on "friendliness, intelligence, kindness, 'hard-workingness,' good looks, cleanliness and honesty." He found that the "Cockney voices receiv[ed] *negative* evaluations for virtually every scale, and the standard-accented voices *positive* ones," even for subjects who were themselves Cockney speakers (Hudson 1980, 204). In other words, lower-class English people associated ideal personality characteristics with the prestige-accent category and not with their own ingroup, which presumably defined their own preference category (at least in terms of social interaction, etc.). This study, of course, may merely indicate that Cockney speakers decided to give the "right" answer—the socially accepted one—to this question, despite their own views being different. But even if this is the case, the study still shows that the effect of prestige categorization is strong, and that logically unrelated properties—intelligence, kindness, good looks, and so on—tend to cluster together and be attributed collectively to high-status individuals. It should be clear that this has consensual or conformist consequences.

I noted above that the schema is structured into a default hierarchy and the prototype is the result of putting all the defaults in place. Yet this is only partly true. While one set of defaults in a schema defines one prototype, for any given lexical item, there may be a series of prototypes, which are themselves arranged in a default hierarchy. Indeed, the example of the pet cat and stray cat indicates just this. The pet cat is the default prototype for "cat." But there are distinct prototypes for "pet cat" and "stray cat." For instance, perceptually, a stray cat has matted or patchy hair, no collar, a thin body, etc. This is important because precisely the same sort of hierarchizing of prototypes occurs in some politically consequential areas, most obviously racism.

What people call stereotypes are largely a subset of prototypes; however, there are some stereotypes that would not count as prototypical. Specifically, a stereotype is a set of properties that is attributed to members of a particular ethnic group. A prototype is a set of properties that is automatically triggered when a particular lexical item is accessed. The prototype is overridden (perhaps replaced by another prototype) only in special circumstances. Again, the prototype is the default. When a stereotype is a default, then it is a prototype; some stereotypes, however, are not defaults. Rather than being triggered automatically, and overcome only in special circumstances, they are triggered only in special circumstances.

To rephrase it, there is a difference between functionalized and nonfunctionalized stereotypes. There are stereotypes about almost every group in the world, but most of these are not socially functionalized—or essentialized, which is to say, generalized as relevant in all contexts. For example, there are stereotypes about Swedish, German, and French women. In terms of social consequences, though, these are not in any way comparable to, say, stereotypes about black women. Socially, the difference is between functionalized and nonfunctionalized stereotypes, stereotypes that operate to define widespread social hierarchies and stereotypes that do not. In terms of the formal operation of human cognition, this difference seems to be largely a matter of "context-bound access" versus "context-free access," that is, nonprototypical stereotypes versus prototypical ones. While various stereotypes about Germans exist (for instance, that they are totalitarians), outside a small group of people who particularly dislike or distrust Germans—and for whom the stereotype is, in effect, socially functionalized—it seems unlikely that any of these stereotypes is the default understanding of a German. Rather, special circumstances are needed in order for this stereotype to be triggered. Suppose Jones is introduced to Helmholtz. It is unlikely that Jones will activate anything that could be referred to as a "stereotype." He or she will, of course, activate a prototype, which includes such properties as "speaks German." But imagine Helmholtz becomes extremely stern and orders Jones to do things when they are supposedly collaborating on some project. Jones may then activate the Nazi stereotype. This contrasts rather sharply with the way in which antiblack, anti-Jewish, or sexist stereotypes operate. In each of these cases, some stereotype is likely to be accessed right at the outset, as the default prototype. Once activated, moreover, it is likely to be far more tenacious, to trigger confirmatory bias, and so on.

One way of understanding this difference is in terms of prototypical humanness, as discussed in the preceding chapter. White people, whatever their national origin, are first of all understood as human (at least by other white people, but also to some extent by nonwhites, as noted earlier). In other words, they first of all trigger the "human" prototype. This may be conceived of as "augmentable" by regional characteristics. For example, the prototypical human would include such underspecified properties as "speaks prototypical human language," with such European languages as English, German, and French available for insertion. Put differently, insofar as ethnic characteristics enter, they do so within an encompassing, human prototype (much as differences between robins and sparrows enter under an encompassing "bird" prototype). It is only under special circumstances that a German, for example, would be shifted out of the human prototype to some ethnic prototype. For blacks, however, the process is precisely the reverse (much as it is for an ostrich or a penguin relative to the bird prototype). It may be possible for a white person eventually to understand an individual black in relation to the human prototype, as specific (humanizing) information displaces stereotype properties (see Holland et al. 1987, 219, 221), but the process begins with the stereotypical properties.

The point may be illustrated by considering the Oklahoma City bombing. As in any case of this sort, investigators were rightly concerned with individuals seen at or near the building that day. One report explained that people had seen several men in Arab dress present there. The implication was obvious: these Arabs may have been responsible. Needless to say, no one remarked on the fact that far more people wearing Western clothing were seen at the building. This is partly a matter of saliency. Yet it is also a matter of the way prototype triggering operates differently in these two instances. In the case of the Arabs, the first prototype triggered is ethnic and includes such properties as "terrorist." As for the European-Americans, the first prototype triggered is "human." (Despite the fact that over the last two centuries, Europeans have far outpaced all other groups in human slaughter. Statistically speaking, when innocent people die, the default suspects should be white.)

As already indicated, even socially functionalized prototypes or stereotypes are not singular. There are often several distinct prototypes for any given outgroup (compare Hamilton and Trolier 1986, 139). These, too, may be arranged in a default hierarchy or may be a function of other variables beyond the one that defines the ingroup/outgroup division. The most important variables of the latter sort appear to be categories that themselves define consequential ingroup/outgroup divisions: age, sex, and economic status. Consider black prototypes. Clearly, these differ for children, adults, and elderly persons, men and women, rich and poor. The adult black man, for one, falls into a small number of prototypes, the most prominent of which are probably athlete/entertainer, street criminal, and unemployed loafer, with all three marked by a high degree of sexual activity—if positive, high sexual abilities; if negative, sexual aggressiveness tending toward rape. The adult black woman also falls into a small number of prototypes, prominently prostitute and welfare mother, but also something along the lines of an aggressive professional advanced due to pugnacity and affirmative action. The most common prototype for the older, postsexual black woman appears to be the competent, stern grandmother. Note that each of these prototypes includes defaults as well. For example, the default "family life" for the welfare mother is "abandoned by (irresponsible) black lover, to whom she was not married." (I am drawing primarily on my own personal sense of common prototypes. This delimitation is, therefore, highly tentative and needs to be replaced by more accurate formulations based on empirical research. Currently, however, such research is sparse—as Hamilton and Trolier [1986, 137] have stressed.)

What seems to happen in stereotypical thinking is something along the following lines. Jones, who is white, sees a black person, Smith. That person's sex, age, and apparent economic status serve as "probes" to isolate the relevant prototype from Jones's lexicon. If Smith is an older black woman, his tendency may be to assume that she is a stern grandmother. If Smith is a young black man, casually dressed, sitting on a park bench, his tendency may be to assume that Smith is irresponsible and has lost his job. These prototypes exert pressure on Jones's understanding of and response to Smith, even after he gains individuating and stereotype-falsifying information about Smith (say, that Smith is well employed, but has the day off).

One thing that must be stressed about all this is that it is in no way dependent on self-conscious beliefs. It took considerable psychological research and theorization to posit and define prototypes. They are not immediately evident via introspection. Their operation is almost entirely nonconscious. But they are central to any understanding of the world. Who would say that they believe birds are robins? No one. But in looking at birds, one's mind first of all refers them to robins (and a few other prototypical birds) for comparison. The same sort of thing happens with people.

LEXICAL TOPICALIZATION AND MOOD

Thus far it has been assumed that the information included in any lexical entry in the mind is fully specified in terms of content, attitude, and the like, yet this may not in fact be the case. It may be that schemas first of all include some focal topic, which is then specifiable in terms of a series of variables. The same holds for prototypes and even exempla. For instance, the prototype for "Jew" may include some topicalizing element along the lines of "money." This topicalization may be specified into "greedy and cheating" or "good at business," depending on shifts in attitude. Similarly, "woman" might include the topicalizing element "feeding." This has a number of consequences, most via other topicalizing elements. With a second topicalizing element, "child care," it is linked to breast-feeding and other maternal activities, as well as oedipal imagoes. With a different second element, "housewife," it is linked to spousal duties, such as cooking—but also, perhaps, to providing emotional "nurturance."

There are several outcomes of this analysis. First, it indicates that any given individual may vary in his or her attitude toward a particular group (say, Jews), or have different attitudes toward individual members of that group, while consistently maintaining a coherent, underlying (stereotypical) view of that group and its members as a whole. In addition, emotive attitudes toward a group or its members may be highly unstable. A positive attitude toward group members, then, does not in any way point to an absence of prejudice. Indeed, it is likely to indicate only a temporarily benevolent attitude. As a result, any positive attitude may readily shift into a negative one, with the underlying representational content of the two (diametrically opposed) attitudes remaining substantially the same. John H. Duckitt (1992) backs this up: a "positive outgroup stereotype can shift rapidly and easily to become extremely negative with a change in circumstances" (157). Ortony, Clore, and Collins (1988) make the same general point as well, explaining that Mary may like John when she links him with her "scholar" prototype and dislike John when she links him with her "pedant" prototype (160). Here too the representational content hardly varies, but the feelings are contradictory. One implication of this is that an ideological "critique" that sets out merely to elevate a positive attitude over a negative one (for example, that women are "nurturant," not "devouring") is likely to do nothing more than reinforce the shared stereotypical content of the two attitudes, thereby worsening the racism or sexism it was intended to undermine.

It is worth noting that attitudinal shifts of this sort may be a matter of broader subjective well-being, with no initial bearing on the object-group in question. Studies by Esses, Haddock, and Zanna (1994) indicate that mood may be an important determinant of the way in which people specify stereotype characteristics. "When people are in a negative mood, they are likely to interpret their stereotypes of certain groups in a particularly unfavorable light" (98). Conversely, "satisfaction with self [is] associated with more positive ethnic attitudes" (Duckitt 1992, 172). This implies that part of the virulence of racism during certain periods has nothing to do with the people who are the object of that racism, not even with the racist's initial imagination of those people. In other words, it is often assumed that an increase in antiblack racism must be founded on something relating to blacks—their negative portrayal in films or television, a prejudicial use of crime statistics by prominent politicians, or a demagogue's appeal to white self-interest in a tightening economy. All these things are, of course, relevant; however, it seems that a significant part of the virulence of a person's racist beliefs is simply a function of his or her independent sense of well-being. The worse one feels, for whatever reason, the more likely one is to adopt hateful versions of stereotypes.

This is one of the reasons why panic tends to foster racism, authoritarianism, and more generally, consent and conformism—a point that is deeply consequential for U.S. society today. As Susan Douglas (1997a) has maintained, the news media are largely driven by the dictum, "If it bleeds, it leads," and are filled with sensationalistic stories of crime and disaster. This "body-bag journalism bludgeons the viewer into a state of cynicism, resignation, and fear." These "sentiments . . . serve a conservative agenda," at least in part, because they lead people to shift from positive to negative attitudes in their beliefs or prototypes. This is most obvious in the case of race, but it applies to a wide range of social phenomena. Everything from places to institutions to people are conceived of via topics inflected by attitudes. As attitudes in general become bleaker, people are more likely to shift to negative specifications of topics across the board. Douglas argues that "the more TV you watch, the more inclined you are to exaggerate the level of crime in society, and to exaggerate your own vulnerability to crime." In consequence, "people who watch a lot of TV are much more likely to favor punitive approaches to crime—such as building more prisons and extending the death penalty—than are light viewers." Presumably, part of what is going on here is that panic leads people to specify crime-related topics in the most negative and dehumanizing way. This, in turn, leads to the advocacy of the harshest and most authoritarian responses. (For a summary of research linking authoritarian convictions to fear of a hostile world, see Duckitt 1992, 207 ff.)

Suppose one topic for "criminals" is "illness," for example. In a positive mood, one might envision an emotionally tortured man or woman, overcome by mental illness as if by some alien force, committing a crime against his or her will; one might even imagine the origins of this illness in his or her own suffering and mistreatment as a child. One might then respond to this by attempting to cure the illness, thereby viewing the response to crime as "treatment" or "rehabilitation." In contrast, in a negative mood, one might conceive of the criminal as akin to a rabid animal, totally overcome by disease, with no separate and human consciousness—incurable, dangerous, contagious, with all that this implies for punitive response. The two views share a common topicalization, differing primarily in emotional attitude.

Beyond single lexical entries and their internal structure, relations among entries—especially those relations defined by lexical domains—are crucial for consent as well. A domain (sometimes called a "semantic field") is a set of linked or coordinated lexical items such that each item in the domain is partially defined by reference to all the others, often by way of some superordinate term. "Monday," "Tuesday," and so forth, for instance, all fall into the domain of days of the week. Likewise, the domain of intelligence might run from "stupid" through "brilliant"—to take a looser scale of degrees, rather than a fully specified set of discrete elements. (Precisely how such a domain is defined will vary from idiolect to idiolect, from person to person.)

The most obvious relevance of domains to an understanding of ideology comes in the definition of problematics. Take the domain "types of government." It seems that most people in the United States tacitly define this domain by reference to two subdomains: totalitarianism and capitalism/democracy. This domain underlies and permits the standard problematic regarding socialism as a form of totalitarianism.

Such a literal or direct operation of domains is, however, not the only way in which these structures bear on ideology. In fact, the metaphorical use of domains is as significant and widespread, if not more so. One of the most common cognitive processes is the mapping of one domain onto another, such that the first serves as a way of structuring and understanding the second. (The most famous discussions of this general phenomenon are by Lakoff and Johnson 1980, and Lakoff and Turner 1989; the following analysis is indebted to their work.) This is "cognitive modeling," and it is perhaps the most consequential way in which domains enter into the generation of consent.

The division of society into ingroups and outgroups, as discussed above, often involves an identification of the ingroup with "human" and the outgroup with "nonhuman." At the very least, it involves identifying members of the ingroup as more prototypically human than members of the outgroup. This is particularly the case when the groups in question are defined and hierarchized by putative essences. Borrowing a term from Max Weber, I will refer to ingroup/outgroup sets of this sort as "status groups," sometimes referring to the putative essences as "status categories." (For Weber's definition, see Weber 1968, 932; for discussion, see Wallerstein in Balibar and Wallerstein 1991, 187–203.)

Status groups involve a sort of ideological contradiction, and thus create a problem for the dominant ideology. The members of status groups are all human, yet some are less human than others or not human at all. Status groups must, by definition, fall within a common domain, "human." But status group stratification contradicts such commonality. Status groups cannot be understood—and differentiated—on the basis of shared properties, nor can status group hierarchies be justified on that basis. For example, if whites are to be owners and blacks are to be slaves, and if there is to be widespread consent to this stratification, then "black" and "white" cannot simply be perceived as alternatives within the domain of "human." If men are to be doctors or business executives and women are to be nurses or housewives, and if there is to be broad consent to this stratification, then "man" and "woman" cannot simply be alternatives within the domain of "human." The schemas and prototypes of "black" and "white," "man" and "woman," cannot be defined primarily through their shared, human properties.

Now, if blacks (or Jews, gays, or women) are not seen primarily as instances of human, they must be understood by reference to some other lexical structures that in addition relate the oppressed group to the oppressor in an appropriate way, in keeping with social stratification. That is, these various structures must form a more encompassing domain, which includes the domain of the human as one part—for the dominant group (white, male, straight, or whatever) must occupy the definitive "human" position in that more encompassing domain. There have been two major domains on which elites have drawn in this way: maturity and animacy. These domains have been used to model status groups both cross-culturally and transhistorically. They are no less prominent today than they were in the past, and they function no less crucially in defining and sustaining social and political stratification.

The domain of maturity is defined by a scale running from childhood through adulthood to old age. The domain of animacy is defined by a scale running from the animal through the human to the angelic/demonic (or superhuman). Each position in the scale provides a potential model for any given status group, with the center point or "standard" reserved for the dominant group. In keeping with the preceding discussion of attitude and topic in group bias, each model involves a negative and positive version. There are, for example, distinct negative and positive models drawn from childhood. Finally, while in principle anyone might adopt any of these models, there is a tendency for particular models to be associated with particular political orientations. Thus, the maturity domain as a whole tends to be the province of liberals, while the animacy domain is standard in right-wing or "conservative" thought.

Before going on to explore these domains in detail, it is worth remarking on the special place of women in status group modeling. In every society of which I am aware, the oppression of women is of the longest standing historically. As such, it is the most fundamental ideologically. The division into male and female is, in a sense, basic to the determination of hierarchized status groups; for instance, it precedes and provides a precedent for racial divisions, as Ashis Nandy has studied in detail (see 1983, 4–11, and 1987, 38). It is similar to these other divisions in that it, too, is regularly modeled on schemas and prototypes drawn from the domains of maturity and spirituality. Nevertheless, it is different in that it often enters into the modeling of those other divisions as well. When colonized people are assimilated to children, to cite one case, they are often simultaneously conceived of as feminine, due it seems to the prior assimilation of women to children. While I will not go into this at any length in what follows, it is important to recognize that the relation between a given model and status group (such as children and Africans) may be mediated by the more long-standing relation between that model and the status group of women.

THE DOMAIN OF MATURITY

The less extreme, and thus less destructive, of the two domains is that of maturity, which as already noted, encompasses models of childhood, adulthood, and old age. (In isolating and examining this domain, I have drawn heavily on Ashis Nandy's pathbreaking study of colonialism, *The Intimate Enemy* [1983, 11–18].) Adulthood is, of course, the standard by which the others are measured, and it is the model for the dominant group. Again, there are attitudinal divisions in the remaining groups; these correspond to further age gradations. Specifically, the *childhood* model is regularly split into the "innocent prepubescent," who requires loving guidance, and the "delinquent adolescent," who requires firm discipline. Old

Figure 1. Maturity

PREPUBESCENT	WISE ELDER
Innocent, asexual or presexual, naive, intellectually limited, no internalized morality but open to guidance, playful, friendly, cute, chattering	Wise, asexual or postsexual, above both morality and instinct, supramundane, antilogical, recondite or silent, benevolent
Africans, women	Asians, women, peasants
Benevolent paternalism	Romantic exclusion
"Soft" or ideological liberalism	Romantic liberalism

ADULT

ADOLESCENT	SENILE DECADENT
Scheming, compulsively sexual, intellectually limited (though less so), in rebellion against guiding parental morality, aggressive, unfriendly, inscrutably silent, ugly or powerfully sexual	Sexually desiccated, feeble, sly, perverse, physically exhausted, mentally dull, noncontagiously ill, isolated, illogical, incoherent, rambling, malevolent
Asians, Africans, women, workers	Asians, Arabs, aristocrats
Punitive paternalism	Telic exclusion
"Tough" or pragmatic liberalism	Revolutionary liberalism

age is likewise divided into what might be called "the wise elder" and "the senile decadent." (For a tabulation of properties, most common status groups, and associated political views for all models of both domains, see figures 1 and 2.)

The infantile model yields a conception of a status group that is asexual or presexual, naive, intellectually limited to basic studies, lacking an internalized morality yet fundamentally good-natured and thus inclined to follow parental guidance, playful and friendly, chattering, and cute. The adolescent model, in contrast, is highly and compulsively sexual, clever or cunning, still intellectually limited (though somewhat less so), actively rebellious against parental authority and morality, aggressive and unfriendly, inscrutably silent, and either ugly or powerfully sexually attractive.

It is not difficult to see that the former is one of the most persistent models for women in our culture. It leads to the conception of women as pure and fragile girls capable of some education in the simpler and more humanistic areas, but easily overtaxed by mental labor; lacking an autonomous superego (as stressed by Freud), although open to the guidance of a father or husband; and so on. Indeed, whole areas of today's culture, from codes of chivalry to matters of etiquette, are closely linked with this notion of women.

But women are not the only status group assimilated to prepubescent children. As Nandy has pointed out, "What was childlikeness of the child and childishness of the immature adults now also became the lovable and unlovable savagery of primitives and the primitivism of subject [that is, colonized] societies" (1983, 15–16); "The culture of the colonizer became the prototype of a mature, complete, adult civilization while the colonized became the mirror of a more simple, primitive, childlike cultural state" (1987, 38). This is the view of Africans as happy, banjo-playing folk, apt for a grade school education only (compare Rodney 1972, 243), friendly and loquacious. The prominent nineteenth-century naturalist Louis Agassiz, for one, maintained that blacks are "indolent, playful . . . imitative, subservient, good natured, versatile, unsteady in their purpose, devoted, affectionate," and thus, "may but be compared to children" (quoted in Gould 1981, 48). Putting the matter and its consequences more bluntly, Cecil Rhodes insisted that "the native is to be treated as a child and denied franchise" (quoted in Nandy 1987, 58).

These are not, of course, the only views of women and Africans as children. In times of peaceable relations, blacks may be readily conceived of as innocents; in periods of rebellion, this is more difficult. The same is true of women. As already noted, attitudes toward outgroups alter drastically with circumstances. John H. Duckitt (1992) remarks that "to the extent that members of the subordinate group accept their inferiority and respectfully acquiesce in their oppression, members of the dominant group may experience positive affect toward them" (101). But relations are not always so irenic. When the childhood model is invoked in less harmonious times, which is to say, with a negative attitude, these groups are assimilated to adolescents.

Before going on, it is worth stopping for a moment to consider the stereotyping of adolescents in contemporary society. As one recent study of "Media Myths about Teenagers" put it, adolescents are themselves misperceived as "violent, reckless, hypersexed . . . obnoxious, ignorant" (Males 1994, 8), to which could be added sullen, devious, and other characteristics. Unsurprisingly, adolescents—like women and blacks—are far more likely to be the victims than the perpetrators of violence and sexual abuse, as Mike Males demonstrates. They are, moreover, disproportionately punished. Males and Faye Docuyanan (1996) report that "in California, studies by the state corrections department show that youths serve sentences 60 percent longer than adults for the same crimes" (24). In short, this "adolescent" model has little relation to adolescents themselves, and is rather a reflection of the denigratory ideology that accompanies the parent/child hierarchy in society.

There are many instances of the use of adolescence as a model for essentialized outgroups. The unconstrained sexuality of women, their immorality, their wiles and inscrutability—so tirelessly stressed in misogynist literature—are all linked with this model. Even more obviously, blacks are frequently assimilated to delinquents. Hence, referring primarily to blacks, G. Stanley Hall, the most prominent psychologist in the United States at the beginning of the twentieth century, wrote that "most savages in most respects are children or . . . more properly, adolescents" (quoted in Gould 1981, 116). Asians are the racial group most consistently understood historically in terms of adolescence—from their decadent sensual luxuriance to their amorality and legendary inscrutability. As Stephen Gould (1981) observes, a number of thinkers have been completely explicit about identifying different categories of adult nonwhites with different categories of white youth. Étienne Serres, a famous French medical anatomist, saw adult blacks as comparable to white children and adult Mongolians as comparable to white adolescents (ibid., 40). The Irish, too, have been regularly understood in these terms. For example, this view was repeatedly articulated by John Milton, who defended the domination of Ireland, including Cromwell's brutal policies, in part by reference to the parental duties of English civilization (see ibid., 663–64).

The innocent, infantile model dictates loving guidance, generosity, and compassion. The well-known nineteenth-century naturalist John Bachman wrote: "In intellectual power the African is an inferior variety of our species. His whole history affords evidence that he is incapable of self-government. Our child that we lead by the hand, and who looks to us for protection and support is still of our own blood notwithstanding his weakness and ignorance" (quoted in ibid., 70). The adolescent model, in contrast, counsels unbending discipline, stringency, and authoritarianism—

"tough love" as it might be called now. The infantile model leads to "benevolent paternalism" and is most often employed by "soft" or ideological liberals (those who claim to place liberal principles above utilitarian concerns). The adolescent model, on the other hand, leads to a form of "punitive paternalism" and is the standard model for "tough" or pragmatic liberalism (which allows liberal principle to be qualified by practical concerns). Though the rhetoric and certain specific beliefs have changed over a hundred years, the use of both models regarding minorities and women remains widespread, if usually somewhat more covert, as will be seen in the discussion of Alan Paton below.

At the other end of the domain of maturity, one finds the models of wise elder and senile decadent. The former characterizes members of a target status group as asexual or postsexual. Neither driven by instinct nor governed by a legalistic morality, they have transcended both, and have achieved a sort of wisdom that goes beyond mechanical and pragmatic social ethics. They are isolated from society, not due to a rebellious and anarchic temperament but rather to a disinterested distance from the quotidian and mundane, a distance that allows them to maintain a state of serenity. They have achieved understanding that goes beyond both practical life and mere reason—indeed, they are often entirely nonlogical, and thus all the more profound. Most often, they are physically undeveloped, and either silent or brilliantly, if perhaps incomprehensibly, loquacious.

The senile model draws on many of the same themes, with the attitude and evaluative presuppositions changed. In this case, members of the target status group are sexually desiccated, capable only of feeble, perverse excitement. Their physical exhaustion and mental torpor remove them from both instinct and morality, though they seek the regeneration of normal adult instinct through twisted means. They are isolated from society in a dull-witted indifference. They say nothing, or ramble incoherently, lacking logical capacities.

The most obvious and common use of both models is for Asians. As, for example, Nandy has shown, Indian society was regularly viewed as "senile and decrepit" by British colonizers (1987, 39), and the idea of declining age was frequently projected onto Indians themselves (see 1983, 17–18), all in the service of the colonial project. While Nandy does not detail the particulars of this projection, they are nonetheless clear. In its negative version, the Indian or other easterner—including, in this case, Arabs—is viewed as typically irrational and torpid, incapable of raising him or herself from mindless drudgery, except when seeking feeble gratification in decadent Eastern practices, such as pederasty (on the putative "lechery, debauchery, sodomy" of Arabs, see Said 1978, 62).

More generally, this negative model takes part in a telic emplotment of history in which the dominant group mythicizes its own political and economic ascendency—"Asians were dominant at the dawn of time, but now they are declined into the vale of years, while we Europeans are young and vigorous; the burden of bringing civilization to its culminating perfection is on our shoulders," and so forth. (On the notion of telic emplotment, see Hogan 1990, 47–49.) This model, then, is not only invoked by the British in India but also by bourgeois writers discussing the (decadent) aristocracy. The political practices associated with this model may be characterized as "telic exclusion," for they operate to eliminate the group in question from political, social, and economic power, while portraying that exclusion as inevitable historical progress. As this view is most important in periods of political change (such as during the shift from feudalism to capitalism, during the establishment of colonial domination, and so on), the political orientation associated with it is best referred to as "revolutionary liberalism."

The positive version of this model is perhaps more common in elite circles today. Again, Asians form the most obvious group to which it is applied. While the Middle East is essential to the senile model, interestingly, it is rarely understood in terms of aged wisdom. Thus the primary groups conceived of in these terms are South and East Asians. This is the view of Indian gurus and Japanese Zen masters generalized as the character of a culture. In this model, the antirational, contemplative, recondite wisdom of the East is elevated above the mundane and rational science of the West. While this notion was perhaps most popular during the late 1960s, it is common enough at present, displayed prominently in a range of outlets from the writings of orientalists, to travel programs, to popular cinema and television.

Other status groups have been depicted in these terms as well, most obviously women. Indeed, certain feminists have been advocates of this view. The special wisdom of women's antirational "intuition," as well as their putative deeper human understanding and removal from the petty competitiveness of everyday life, are part of this model.

Another status group variously understood in these elevated terms is the peasantry. While the delinquent model has had widespread application to a nascent proletariat, and while the senile model has been employed in connection with the aristocracy (the proletariat and aristocracy being the two main enemies of the rising bourgeoisie), the wise model has been nostalgically invoked with respect to a vanishing peasantry. This nostalgic attitude can be clearly seen in (disaffected petit bourgeois) intellectuals and writers such as William Butler Yeats and in a number of the romantics who seek a lost wisdom in the folk.

When applied to the peasantry, this elevating view is associated with what classical marxist thinkers refer to as "romantic anticapitalism." A more general term might be "romantic liberalism," for this sort of modeling implies a "romantic antipatriarchy," a "romantic anticolonialism," and so on, all of which operate to romanticize the group in question—while still excluding its members from political, economic, and social power. In keeping with this, the political practices connected with this model are best labeled "romantic exclusion."

THE DOMAIN OF ANIMACY

The second domain is, again, divisible into the subhuman or animal, the human, and the superhuman or angelic/demonic. The dominant group is understood as human and the various dominated groups are understood as sub- or superhuman. The "animal" model is perhaps the one most commonly recognized. It is roughly divisible into the (positive) "work animal" and the (negative) "wild animal," but the two share a majority of properties. Members of status groups understood as bestial are thus viewed as unusually strong, perhaps athletic, and powerfully built. They are highly potent and sexually active, and their reproduction—physically signaled by large and prominent genitalia—is unconstrained by law or morals, except insofar as instinct produces moral effects, as when animal mothers care for their offspring. The intellectual capacities of members of this status group are almost nil, certainly below those of children. They are also judged as being less individual—a notion that actually makes no sense; it is merely a projection of the racist inability to distinguish individuals in other races (see Gerbrands 1978, 150).

In its negative or wild version, this model characterizes members of the relevant status group as violent—even rabid or mad—beasts who are prone

Figure 2. Animacy

WORK ANIMAL	ANGEL
Strong, athletic, highly potent and sexually active, sexually well endowed, lacking morality (acts by instinct), very poor intellect, less individual	Selfless, devoted to the well-being of others, curative, desexualized, hypermoral, with a spiritualized intellect
Blacks, Irish, workers	Women
Benevolent exploitation	Romantic exploitation
"Soft" or pragmatic conservatism	Romantic conservatism

HUMAN

WILD ANIMAL	DEVIL
Violent, prone to anarchic destruction and killing, otherwise as above	Devoted to the destruction of humanity, bearers of physical, mental, or spiritual disease, contagious, seductive, with an evil and manipulative intellect, identifiable only by a secret mark
Blacks, Irish	Jews, heretics, "witches," gays
Punitive extermination	Telic extermination
"Tough" or ideological conservatism	Revolutionary conservatism

to unpredictable destruction and must be caged or killed. In its positive version, it portrays these people as solid, if dumb workers, who must be fed, harnessed, prodded, and whipped, but can work like an ox. Both versions lead to an almost complete disregard for the lives of the people in question.

Historically, this model underwrote slavery and certain aspects of colonialism in Africa. Such classic racist texts as Arthur de Gobineau's (1856) *The Moral and Intellectual Diversity of Races* are explicit on the point. Thus he maintains that "the dark races are the lowest on the scale. The shape of the pelvis has a character of animalism" (443); they have a particularly acute sense of smell (444); their "anger is violent, but soon appeased" (445), and so they kill "without much provocation or subsequent remorse" (446); they lack any sense of vice and virtue (446), and so on—all clearly characteristics derived from a partially explicit animal model. In keeping with this, in his introduction to de Gobineau, H. Hotz maintained that the "Black Races" have a "Feeble" intellect and "Animal Propensities" that are "Very strong" (94). As Sander Gilman (1985) notes, George Louis Leclerc, Count of Buffon, one of the founders of anthropology, went so far as to claim that blacks regularly copulate with apes (212). Frank Reeves (1983) cites one eighteenth-century writer who insisted that blacks have "bestial fleece, instead of hair" (39). The animality of blacks has been a commonplace of ultraright and fascist groups in the twentieth century also (see the bizarre claims cited in McCuen 1974, 56, 59–60, 62).

Unfortunately, this model extends beyond the ultraright. Frantz Fanon (1967) found that a majority of the whites he interviewed in the 1940s had the following associations with the word "Negro": "biology, penis, strong, athletic, potent, boxer, Joe Louis, Jesse Owens, Senegalese troops, savage, animal," and so on (166). Forty years later, Teun van Dijk (1987) did research on common views of a range of racial minorities in the Netherlands and United States. He found that they were widely perceived as prolific, aggressive, violent, criminal, dirty, lazy, and noisy (59). Thus, both studies elicited a combination of adolescent and animal characteristics.

The nearly complete disregard for the lives of black people, so painfully evident in the U.S. judiciary and police, indicates that this model is a frequent guide to action as well—whether in the casual brutalization or murder of blacks by police, or the refusal of white juries to think of brutalized or murdered blacks as humans and so to punish the malefactors. The Amadou Diallo case, both the police action and the jury's decision, is the most obvious instance of this, but it is far from the only one. As noted in chapter 1, Salim Muwakkil (1997) has stressed that "police are using deadly force more and more frequently" against blacks (16), and cites Amnesty International reports on police brutality in New York City, Chicago, and Los Angeles. He does not need to illustrate the case by reference to Amadou Diallo. Rather, he points to "18-year-old Tyrone Lewis, an unarmed black man" who was "shot and killed . . . during a routine traffic stop"; "Joseph Gould, an unarmed homeless black man . . . shot to death" in Chicago; "Aaron White . . . shot to death" after "a traffic accident"; "James Cooper, a black 19-year-old . . . shot to death . . . during a traffic stop in Charlotte, N.C."; and Jonny Gamage, a "31-year-old black businessman" who "died in the custody of five police officers after being stopped for 'driving erratically' " (16–17).

In keeping with this, Samuel Gross and Robert Mauro (1989) point out that "blacks and other racial minorities are far more likely than whites to be the victims of homicides" (43). What is worse, "the risk of a death sentence was far lower for those suspects charged with killing black people . . . than for those charged with killing whites." In Georgia, for example, "those who killed whites were almost ten times as likely to be sentenced to death as those who killed blacks" (44). Moreover, "blacks who killed whites were several times more likely to be sentenced to death than whites who killed whites" (45).

The same model has operated with respect to laborers—and to the Irish, especially in the late nineteenth and early twentieth centuries, when the Irish were both colonized subjects and workers low in the microhierarchization of the working class. As Perry Curtis (1921) has demonstrated, during this period, the Irishman was repeatedly represented as "a dangerous apeman" (vii); "some Victorians . . . went further by discovering features in Irish character which they took to be completely simian" (2). In 1860, Charles Kingley described the peasants of Mayo as "white chimpanzees," and two years later, an article in Punch posited that the Irish were the missing link "manifestly between the Gorilla and the Negro" (quoted in ibid., 100). Later in the century, the only chimpanzee in the London Zoo was named "Paddy" (101). Indeed, the connection with blacks was explicit, as the Irish were often referred to as "white negroes" (1), "Africanoid" (20), and the like. The British shoot-to-kill policy in Northern Ireland— whether official, unofficial, or merely a matter of unreflective common practice—suggests that the bestial model still operates with respect to the Irish, at least some Irish Catholics (on the shoot-to-kill policy, see P. Jenkins 1988; Green 1988).

In short, like the other models discussed earlier, the bestial one provides a cognitive structure that leads individuals to enact and even extend discriminatory practices. These practices, in turn, reproduce aspects of racial and economic stratification, undermining modes of identification, empathy, and solidarity that would work against such stratification.

As divisions by spirituality are more rigidly differential than those by maturity, more extreme in distinguishing dominant and dominated groups, they are best associated not with paternalism and exclusion but with exploitation and extermination (on the difference between the racism of oppression or exploitation and that of extermination, compare Balibar and Wallerstein 1991, 39). The work animal or "beast of burden" model, which has also functioned historically as a model for the laboring classes, is the model of what might be called "benevolent exploitation"—straightforward exaction of labor power, but with the sort of benevolent attitude a farmer typically shows toward work animals. The political orientation associated with this model may be referred to as "soft" or pragmatic conservatism (that is, conservatism that allows the modification of conservative principles by reference to pragmatic considerations—such as the long-term productivity of the workers, general worker satisfaction, and so on; equivalently, "moderate" conservatism). The wild beast model is that of "punitive extermination," which is to say, the physical harm or killing of individuals as "required" by their threatening animal violence, as in lynchings and the sorts of police actions just mentioned. It is linked with "tough" or ideological conservatism (that is, conservatism that does not allow principles to be modified by reference to practical concerns; equivalently, "hardline" conservatism).

The "superhuman" models, "angelic" and "demonic," complete this domain. These models share a characterization of the group as possessing special talents or powers and a related, systematic devotion (positive or negative) to the fate of humanity. The angelic model is the simpler of the two. It depicts members of the relevant status group as selflessly devoted to the well-being of others, with an intelligence that is completely spiritualized, which is to say entirely organized and guided by reference to ministering. Needless to say—despite John Milton's views on the cupidity of angels—members of this group are desexualized; having no selfish desires whatsoever, they cannot be subject to carnal lust. Indeed, it is as if instinct has been replaced by a sort of hyper-moral drive, a drive that takes members of this group beyond mere conformity with moral precepts into a constant pursuit of benevolence.

I know of no status group for which this serves as a model other than that of women. This is the view of woman elevated above man into a sort of spiritual principle. It is the view of woman as the perfect mother, spiritual guide, or in literature, muse. In Christian mythology, this is found most obviously in the Virgin Mary; in European literature, the most famous case is probably Beatrice. Moreover, it is a model that continues to the present day, as various feminist and feminist-inspired analyses of modern literature and popular culture have revealed.

This model is related to that of the wise elder, but is even more constraining. It romanticizes the status group (women) and thus elevates it, but it does so in one area only: moral benevolence. There is no question of intellectual superiority or wisdom, a withdrawal from ordinary life, and such. It entails absolute devotion and selflessness. The political actions associated with this model might be referred to as "romantic exploitation" and the political orientation as "romantic conservatism."

Finally, there is the demonic. Members of a status group understood in terms of this model are usually seen as highly intelligent, extremely sexual, and in some way physically degenerate. But more important, like the Devil who might seduce people into everlasting torment, they are the bearers of some ineradicable suffering. This may be religious error, yet it may equally be a form of physical disease or mental and social degeneracy. In any case, it is something that will destroy humanity. The demonic model in this way incorporates the domain of sickness/health, as does the partially parallel senile decadent model—though in the demonic version, the illness is contagious. Note that the angelic model involves the opposite implication, for the angelic woman is metaphorically—and as a selfless nurse, perhaps even literally—curative. Furthermore, members of such demonized status groups are identifiable only by a secret mark, like Satan with his cloven hoof. They know one another and conspire together. But they are often entirely unrecognizable to outsiders—that is, to "normal" humans. This obscurity is compounded by the fact that they may make use of members of other status groups to do their dirty work.

This paranoic fantasy of fascism and related politics is most often part of a telic emplotment of history in which a dominant group imagines that shadowy figures are seeking the overthrow of the present order, and must be stopped so that the given order may continue and reach its culmination. The activities of these figures, though sometimes only barely discernible, constitute a clear and present danger. Thus, they must be systematically exposed and exterminated. The political behaviors associated with this model may be referred to as "telic extermination" and the political orientation itself as "revolutionary conservatism." The sharpest instance of this is, of course, Nazi Germany, probably the most complete culture of conformism in history.

Jews are the most obvious status group to have been conceived of in these terms. They have been widely viewed as shrewdly intelligent, clannish, and separatist. It is a racist commonplace that they already do conspiratorially control world government and finance, or are quickly maneuvering to do so in the future (see McCuen 1974, 142; Kushener 1989, 37–40; and Holmes 1989, 202–3). In *Mein Kampf*, Adolf Hitler (1940) insisted that "the Jew today is the great agitator for the complete destruction of Germany. Whenever in the world we read about attacks on Germany, Jews are their fabricators" (906). Indeed, more generally, "if . . . the Jew conquers the nations of this world, his crown will become the funeral wreath of humanity" (84).

It is similarly commonplace that Jews are the brains behind the efforts of blacks to destroy civilization (McCuen 1974, 97). One specific threat posed by the Jew is the miscegenation of white and black—one form of undermining consent to racial stratification. As Hitler put it, "It was and is the Jews who bring the negro to the Rhine, always with the same concealed thought and the clear goal of destroying, by the bastardization which would necessarily set in, the white race which they hate" (448–49). Jews have also been widely seen as murderers and rapists (Gilman 1991, 117 ff.; see also Hitler 1940, 448), and the bearers of physical and mental disease, especially the doubly effective syphilis (Gilman 1991, 96).

Most significantly, Jews are not inevitably identifiable. Once they adopt an "assimilated" appearance, all that might remain as an identifying sign is the hidden mark of circumcision. Detlev Peukert (1982) refers to this as "the mythical hate-figure of the essential 'Jew' lurking behind the most disparate surface appearances" (209). In *Mein Kampf*, Hitler (1940) explained that he was slow in recognizing the Jewish threat because "their external appearance had become European and human" (67), and in a related way, he emphasized that they are the true "masters of lying" (313). The most graphic representation of this which I have seen is in a 1972 advertisement for the American Christian Party, in which the headline asks: WHO IS THIS MAN?? He LOOKS like an American/He DRESSES like an American/He SPEAKS the same language as Americans/But . . . HE IS A JEW!/DON'T TRUST HIM!!" (quoted in McCuen 1974, 177).

Of course, Jews have been explicitly linked with Satan as well. Hitler (1940) referred to Jews as "devils incarnate" (82) and maintained that "the personification of the Devil . . . assumes the living appearance of the Jew" (447). The official organ of the Ku Klux Klan averred in 1973 that "Jesus Christ revealed that the Jews . . . are the offspring of Satan" (quoted in McCuen 1974, 12; see also 141).

A number of other groups have been assimilated to the diabolic model, too. Perhaps the most striking case is that of homosexuals, who have been understood as concealed and socially dangerous. Heinrich Himmler feared homosexual deceitfulness and saw homosexuality as a grave threat to the future of the German nation, German culture, and the German people: "If this vice continues, it will be the end of Germany," he warned (quoted in Plant 1986, 89).

Historically, homosexuals were repeatedly linked with heretics and witches, and thus implicitly with Satan. As Louis Crompton (1985) points out, "From the start the medieval and Spanish Inquisitions ranked homosexuals with heretics as a class of persons to be sought out and destroyed" (13). In many countries, "executions for sodomy reached their height during the sixteenth and seventeenth centuries, at the same time as witch hunts and heresy trials" (14). Crompton notes that in his 1748 *The Spirit of the Laws*, Montesquieu recognized the connection and placed homosexuality in the same legal category as heresy and witchcraft (16).

In recent years, the spread of AIDS and its association with homosexuality has revived the use of this model. The paranoic anecdotes one hears—usually with disclaimers—concerning gay men who are intentionally infecting straight women with the virus, the repeated references of the religious right to divine vengeance on Sodom, and even the otherwise prudent and necessary insistence of health officials that one cannot recognize someone who has AIDS, form a coherent and frightening pattern. It goes without saying that this sort of modeling fosters not only consent to but an extension of homophobic discrimination. Indeed, as a number of authors have observed, some recent proposals for dealing with AIDS victims are shockingly reminiscent of Nazism. Gilman (1991), for one, notes that in 1987, "a number of West German municipal officials had approved the idea for a new 'AIDS-camp' based on the plans for the infamous concentration camp at Sachsenhausen" (227).

CRY, THE BELOVED COUNTRY

In order to reveal the nature and function of these models, I have drawn on relatively explicit uses—direct references to blacks as animals or Jews as demons. Nonetheless, these models operate for the most part implicitly, guiding thought and action, fostering consent to and enactment of status hierarchies, in ways of which we are entirely unaware. The unselfconscious operation of these models is, moreover, in many ways more significant than their explicit operation. After all, insofar as racist, sexist, or homophobic thinking is implicit, it is more difficult to recognize, and thus more difficult to counter. It is, in short, more thoroughly conformist.

For this reason, I will conclude by considering a more subtle case of racist modeling: Alan Paton's *Cry, the Beloved Country*. As I have argued elsewhere (Hogan 1992–1993) Paton has genuine sympathy for his main character, the gentle black minister, Stephen Kumalo. But he develops this sympathy in a context that is paternalistic. His attitude recalls John H. Duckitt's (1992) observation that "to the extent that members of the subordinate group accept their inferiority and respectfully acquiesce in their oppression, members of the dominant group may experience positive affect toward them" (101). Paton's own politics, as expressed in the novel, are a version of benevolent paternalistic liberalism, but with distinct punitive elements as well. This combination is unsurprising, as the difference between these views is largely one of attitude relative to topicalization. When he thinks of the slow-witted minister, Paton's attitude is positive and his politics are benevolent; when he thinks of the murderous black gangsters, his attitude is negative and a punitive pragmatism enters—though his overall tendency is to stress the former over the latter.

Paton does not confine the problematic of the novel to his own preferences, however. He extends it slightly beyond the alternatives of ideological and pragmatic liberalism. While he does not include any genuinely *human* alternative, any alternative, such as marxism, that does not distinguish between blacks and whites in terms of these models at all, Paton does incorporate elements of pragmatic and ideological conservatism.

In terms of the domains explored here, then, Paton's presentation of blacks is largely based on the childhood model—both prepubescent and adolescent—with the two versions of the animal model entering at points.

For my purposes, what is important about Paton's use of these domains is that it does not simply involve the use of explicit characterizations of Africans as children or animals but the generation of a broad range of ideas about blacks and whites, about relations between them, as well as a wide variety of images, narrative elements, and so forth, all of which rely implicitly on these models. At each point in the story, as Paton is faced with choices of character and action, the models operate to push his decision in a certain direction. For example, even when the blacks in question are literally adults and the whites are literally children, these models lead Paton to depict the latter as more adult than the former. The operation of these models is so ubiquitous, in fact, that they extend beyond character to setting and imagery as well.

The general argument of the novel, explicit in a treatise by the murdered hero, Arthur Jarvis, is that traditional African society was greatly inferior to Christian, European society. Hence, it was morally right for Europeans to destroy indigenous culture. Europeans erred, however, in failing to replace African barbarity with Christian civilization. As Jarvis puts it, "It was permissible to allow the destruction of a tribal system" consisting in "violence and savagery . . . superstition and witchcraft. . . . But it is not permissible to watch its destruction, and to replace it by nothing," for after all, "we are a Christian people" and as such, "we shall never . . . be able to evade the moral issues." The result of this neglect is that "a whole people [has] deteriorate[d] physically and morally" (Paton 1987, 146), leading to "the deterioration of native family life . . . poverty, slums and crime" (145). That is, whites have not been good parents. They have rightly ended the childish—or perhaps animalistic—ways of the natives, but they have not fulfilled the duty of all parents to educate their children. Jarvis makes the use of this model almost explicit: "Society has always . . . educated its children so that they grow up law-abiding, with socialized aims and purposes" (ibid.), yet Europeans have failed to do this with the natives (146).

To make it clear that Jarvis's views are true—so true that they are shared even by blacks themselves—this excerpt from his treatise is preceded by a testimonial, a letter of praise and gratitude. In keeping with the underlying model of the novel, the letter is "from the secretary of the Claremont African Boys' Club" (144)—another obvious, if implicit, manifestation of the childhood model of blacks. As Reverend Msimangu testifies, "It is not in my heart to hate a white man. It was a white man who brought my father out of darkness" (25), implicitly making his own father a child with respect to the white man. Msimangu goes on to explain that the problem is that this "bringing out of darkness" has been incomplete with most natives. As Jarvis argues, the parental work must be continued and extended.

The idea is taken up later, again indirectly, in the novel's school for the blind. Speaking both literally and metaphorically, Msimangu tells Stephen

Kumalo, "It will lift your spirits to see what the white people are doing for our blind" (71). In the course of the visit to the school, the metaphorical and paternalistic meaning becomes increasingly apparent: "It was white men who . . . came together to open the eyes of black men that were blind" (89). The visit culminates in a church service in which the white man's effort "to open the blind eyes" (90) of Africans is explicitly presented as a matter of religious education—the duty of parents to children.

Moreover, in defining the broader problematic within which he wishes the debate to unfold, Paton does not contrast his view with that of the Communist Party of South Africa (CPSA), African National Congress (ANC), or anyone who might consider blacks to be fully adult, and who might see whites as guilty not of withholding education but of practicing gross brutality. Rather, he goes on to oppose his benevolent paternalism to a politics of benevolent exploitation, based on a bestial model: "We go so far as to credit Almighty God with having created black men to hew wood and draw water for white men" (154). Though Jarvis, and Paton, reject this view, the novel makes clear that it marks out the only real alternative to paternalism; these two positions implicitly define the problematic within which the novel unfolds.

Paton does present a version of ANC and CPSA views, without naming them explicitly, but he does so in such a way as to exclude them from the range of rational discussion. For example, John Kumalo (Stephen Kumalo's "evil" brother) articulates an understanding of South African society that is in keeping with the analyses of the ANC and CPSA—and more important, with the facts of white racism and the exploitation of blacks. But Paton dismisses John as having "a voice to move thousands, with no brain behind it" (183). He also has John betray his brother and nephew, evidently allowing his nephew to die, so that his own son will not go to jail. This reprehensible action serves to undermine any moral status John might have. In this context, John's opinions are well beyond the limits of reasonable discourse. This is relevant here because John is largely presented in terms of the adolescent model—sneaky, deceitful, criminal, disloyal to family. His son is literally a juvenile delinquent, and their similarity in this regard is implicitly stressed by John's behavior during his son's criminal trial. Indeed, John even evidences the sort of sexual promiscuity associated with the adolescent model, for he is living in sin with another woman after having separated from his wife.

This treatment of John is, furthermore, part of an undermining of black leadership of any sort—a necessary consequence of the childhood model of blacks. After all, adults are leaders; children are followers. If blacks are children, then they cannot be leaders. Thus, of the three nonwhite leaders in the book, only "a brown man named Tomlinson" (39) has "brains" (43). Only the man who is half white, in other words, has adult intelligence. In contrast, one white leader, Hoernle, has the best attributes of all three men (46), without their flaws. It is obvious who should be the leader in this context: the fully adult white man, with the half-white man serving as an intermediary to the blacks who have no brains.

The traditional chief in the novel is only marginally better than John. He is assimilated to the infantile model, not the adolescent one, but he is foolish and untutored—not innocent and goodly, like Stephen. Specifically, he spends his day riding about with his counselors and wearing ludicrous clothing (for example, "he wore a fur cap such as they wear in cold countries" [229]). When a surveying team comes to the area, he tries to imitate them, pretending in a decidedly infantile and even embarrassing manner that he is undertaking the same professional task, just as a small child might do.

The explicit arguments of Jarvis/Paton are instantiated in the plot and characterization of the novel as a whole—again, primarily through the development of the childhood model. The African characters are largely divided into childlike innocents, on the one hand, and oversexualized adolescent criminals, on the other—with the men in the latter group being murderers, and the women being prostitutes. In keeping with the broader problematic of the novel, however, there is, again, some use of the animal model. Early in the novel, the reader learns that Stephen Kumalo's wife reacts "with the patient suffering of black women, with the suffering of oxen" (10). Shortly afterward, the reader is told of a "strong smell" in the non-European train carriage (13), a repetition of the racist commonplace that blacks emit an animal-like odor. When Stephen meets his sister, she "looks at him sullenly, like an animal that is tormented" (30); subsequently, she acts out this animalism by falling on the floor and crying "louder and louder" with "no shame" (31). The only clear use of wild animal imagery is with John and his followers, for he has "the voice of a bull or a lion" (36; see also 39, 183), and when he "growls," the people "growl" also. It is not surprising that the passive Mrs. Kumalo is assimilated to a gentle work animal (an ox), while the rabble-rousing ANC-associated John Kumalo is assimilated to the violent and dangerous bull or lion (implicitly, to be hunted and killed by "man").

Yet again, the more common models are drawn from childhood. Stephen is the clearest case of a good child, open to the paternal instruction of whites, such as Jarvis. Right at the outset, the reader is told that "Kumalo's voice rose a little, as does the voice of a child" (13). When someone takes his arm, it is "like walking with a child" (95). When faced with the complexities of trains, buses, and city life, he is overcome with childish panic and "his heart beats like that of a child," until he calls out to the paternal, Christian deity (17). When asked a question, he answers "obediently" (23). And most of all, Stephen is filled with childlike gratitude to kindly, parental white people: "Kumalo's face wore the smile . . . of a black man when he sees one of his people helped in public by a white man" (50–51). At the end of the novel, when he has returned to his village, he "sits there like a child" in a meeting with his Bishop (260).

Even more significantly, Stephen plays with Jarvis's young son as if they were the same age. Indeed, the little boy speaks and acts in a more obviously adult manner than Stephen ever does. While Stephen is continually compared to a child, this child, when dealing with Stephen, is compared to an adult, in keeping with the modeling at the base of the novel: "The small white boy . . . walked over to [Stephen's] house with the assurance of a man, and dusted his feet and took off his cap before entering the house" (248). Consistent with this general relation, Stephen refers to the senior Jarvis's wife as "the mother" (257), and Paton presents an image of all the blacks mourning her death as if she were their mother (258). (It is worth recalling that Jarvis's huge land holdings were simply stolen from these same blacks and that the 1913 Land Act reserved roughly 90 percent of South African land for whites, even though blacks constituted over 75 percent of the population [Simons and Simons 1969, 131]. Given this context, such childlike love seems singularly unlikely.) Finally, when James Jarvis (Arthur Jarvis's father) undertakes to help these Africans, of all the things he could do, his first gesture is the parental act of giving them milk (Paton 1987, 237).

Stephen's daughter-in-law is a sort of transitional case. She has had a child out of wedlock, thus demonstrating the type of unconstrained sexuality associated with the adolescent model. But she has not lost her "dependent and affectionate nature" (247). When they meet, she looks at Stephen "with strange innocence" (113), and when he asks her to join his family, "she clap[s] her hands like a child" (116). She is like the other "natives" on the train, who "talk like children" (220), when she goes to the village, or like the woman who was "more like a child than a woman" (221). She can still be saved. She has almost passed over the threshold into destructive adolescence, yet she maintains enough of her childlike innocence that it is possible to "reclaim" and educate her.

Stephen's son, Absolom, on the other hand, is more clearly adolescent. He has not only fathered an illegitimate child (perhaps even many illegitimate children, with different mothers [68]); he has also committed "the most terrible deed that a man can do. . . . He has killed a white man" (111; those who imagine this to be a peculiarly South African bias should recall that in the United States, the murder of whites is far more severely punished than the murder of blacks [Gross and Mauro 1989, 44]). Absolom is ultimately executed for his crime. But he is only a small part of the problem. Paton's portrayal of "native" men is consistently criminal. The entire country is plagued by "young criminal children" (adolescents, as the novel makes clear), "young men and young girls that went away and forgot their customs and lived loose and idle lives," violent teens who steal, rape, and murder "nearly every day" (22). In keeping with this, Reverend Msimangu laments the "tragic things" about life in South Africa—specifically, that "children break the law, and old white people are robbed and beaten" (26). More details of crimes committed by "our young boys" (44) are subsequently revealed. Most important, one central image in the novel for admirable action in rebuilding society, for aiding blacks, is the reformatory. The relation of this image to the adolescent model is too obvious to require elaboration.

It is perhaps worth mentioning the situation faced by blacks in South Africa in the 1940s when the novel was written; the disabilities affecting blacks included virtual exclusion from land ownership (see Simons and Simons 1969, 131), wages for labor paid at roughly one-tenth the rate of whites (Callinicos 1981, 154), complete political disenfranchisement, and subjection to a range of other economically, psychologically, and physically debilitating laws. It is also worth highlighting that a large number of criminal laws applied to blacks only and that the vast majority of criminal convictions of black people were for violations of those laws. For example, figures from slightly before the events of the novel show that almost 80 percent of black "crime" would not have been crime under a nonracist legal system (ibid., 210). In addition, the remaining crimes of murder and robbery were slight when compared with the vastly greater murder and robbery perpetrated legally by whites. Consider theft. Whites simply stole 90 percent of the land and virtually all the mineral resources—which is to say, virtually all the national wealth. Purses and wallets pilfered by black muggers amounted to almost nothing by comparison. Similar points could be made about murder. It is crucial to keep this in mind in order to recognize fully the degree to which Paton's image of a saving reformatory is the product of a racist cognitive model and not the real conditions in South Africa.

Paton's novel has been widely praised in the United States. For years, it was required reading in many U.S. high schools, and still may be. Only a few years ago, it was made into a major motion picture. In short, this is not some "marginal" racist text. Quite the contrary. In the West, at least—and especially in the United States—it has been widely viewed as a profound and moving exploration of and response to racial problems.

Readers of Paton in the United States will recognize why this is so. The novel largely represents the problematic in which mainstream debates about race have unfolded in this country. Despite the horrible economic deprivation of African Americans, despite the constant and debilitating racism they suffer, despite the facts about crime and punishment discussed in the preceding chapters, the entire debate about race problems in this country attempts to respond to the question, "What is wrong with black people?" The presuppositions of this question are not only empirically false but morally obscene. To make matters worse, the debate itself is polarized between a racist conservatism and a racist liberalism, the former relying on an animal model, the latter relying on a childhood model, in keeping with the preceding analyses and Paton's novel. The Right adopts the view that blacks are subhuman (with, for example, genetically inferior intellectual capacities, according to Richard Hervinstein and Charles Murray in The Bell Curve) and animalistic—"created [by God] . . . to hew wood and draw water for white men" (154), in Paton's phrase. Liberals, in turn, adopt the view that blacks are trapped in a "culture of poverty"—that their "simple system of order and tradition and convention has been destroyed," that they live without socialization and morality, and that is why "our natives today produce criminals and prostitutes and drunkards" (146). In short, the national problematic is limited to precisely the options set out in Paton's novel. This is partly because it relies on the same sorts of cognitive modeling, the same implicit use of the domains of age and animacy, to justify the same type of unjustifiable hierarchy, and to foster not only passive consent but active reproduction of that hierarchy.

AFTERWORD

Working against Injustice

The preceding pages have presented a rather grim picture of human society and the human mind. It is my hope, however, that in clarifying the sources and operation of social acquiescence, they will be of practical value to those who have undertaken the difficult work of struggling against unjust social stratification, the conformity that sustains it, and the consent that reproduces it. On the other hand, the preceding analysis may be so grim that some readers might wonder if the forces fostering consent are just too great to be overcome. Here, a few words of encouragement are in order.

First, while many psychological tendencies push toward conformism, many work against it. Empathy is an obvious case. At least some degree of empathy can be produced simply by deciding to take another person's point of view. Moreover, in many situations, especially when one directly sees another person's suffering, empathic feeling results spontaneously (Davis 1994, 124–25). This is why large areas of ideology (such as cognitive modeling in racism, sexism, and homophobia) must operate to inhibit empathy, for it is a continual threat to oppressive hierarchies that produce great human pain.

Moreover, many social and psychological structures and propensities that seem consensual may be reoriented toward nonconsensual ends. For instance, the operation of cognitive exempla may undermine the most carefully scripted Pentagon propaganda—in part through triggering empathic identification. One need only recall the impact of two famous photographs from the Vietnam War: a naked girl burned by napalm, a blind-folded man shot point blank. Similarly, economic insecurity can not only inhibit but inspire activism—in the context of carefully developed solidarity among those who share that insecurity.

Or consider the conformity that results from the belief that one is alone in holding a particular view. Many people will actually deny the plain evidence of their senses, regarding simple observational matters, in order to make their responses fit with what everyone else is saying (see Biener and Boudreau 1991, 449–51). Related to this, in Stanley Milgram's famous studies of obedience, a significant majority of test subjects were willing to deliver evidently fatal electrical shocks simply because the experimenter told them to do so (ibid., 442–44). What might one possibly do to work against such tendencies? In fact, the answer to this question is remarkably simple: one should visibly dissent, refuse to go along. Lois Biener and Louis Boudreau point out that "the most effective means of undermining the power of . . . authority" is "to provide the subject with disobedient peers" (445). Because of human psychology, consent tends to breed consent. But for the same reasons, dissent tends to breed dissent. "Asch (1955) discovered that the presence of a single deviant from the otherwise unanimous majority reduced the amount of conformity to about one-quarter of what it had been when the [participants] expressed unanimity." Indeed, "regardless of the size of the majority, the presence of a single dissenter always reduced conformity" (457).

For readers who may feel encouraged to take up such dissident work, I include the following—very incomplete—list of outlets for activism. For those who feel strongly that things should change, but also feel overwhelmed by the enormity of the task and multiplicity of different outlets, I might offer one concluding bit of advice. No one can do everything. When considering what sort of activism to undertake, first decide what you are genuinely inclined to do. Don't hold yourself up to an impossible ideal—then you will end up doing nothing. Choose an outlet that you are comfortable with. Whatever you do is good, whether it is organizing a rally or writing letters from your home. There are many types of work that need to be done. As Woody Allen said, if everyone in New York went to the same deli on the same day, there would be chaos. The same is true of activism. Diversity is good, even among dissidents.

American Civil Liberties Union
132 West 43rd
New York, NY 10036–6599
www.aclu.org

American Council for Voluntary
    International Action
1717 Massachusetts Ave., NW
Suite 701
Washington, DC 20036
202-667-8227
www.interaction.org

American Friends Service
    Committee
1501 Cherry
Philadelphia, PA 19102
215-241-7000
www.afsc.org

Americans for Democratic Action
1625 K St., NW
Suite 210
Washington, DC 20006
202-785-5980
adaction.org

Amnesty International
322 Eighth Ave.
New York, NY 10001
www.amnesty.org

Campaign for Labor Rights
1247 E St., SE
Washington, DC 20003
541-344-5410
www.summersault.com/~agi/clr/

Center for Campus Organizing
165 Friend St.
Boston, MA 02114–2025
617-725-2886
cco.org

Committee in Solidarity with the
    People of El Salvador
P.O. Box 1801
New York, NY 10159
212-229-1290
www.cispes.org

Co-op America
1612 K St., NW, #600
Washington, DC 20006
202-872-5307

Democratic Socialists of America
180 Varick
New York, NY 10014
212-727-8610
www.dsausa.org

Economic Democracy Information
    Network
garnet.berkeley.edu:3333/

Gay and Lesbian Alliance against
    Defamation
8455 Beverly Blvd.
Suite 305
Los Angeles, CA
www.glaad.org

The Greens/Green Party USA
P.O. Box 1134
Lawrence, MA 01842
978-682-4353
www.greenparty.org/

Institute for Global
  Communications
www.igc.org

International Human Rights
  Association of American
  Minorities
Suite 253, 919C Albert St.
Regina, SK
S4R 2P6 Canada
306-789-0474
www.ihraam.org

Labor Party
Box 53177
Washington, DC 20009
www.labornet.org/lpa/

NAACP Washington Bureau
1025 Vermont Ave., NW
Suite 1120
Washington, DC 20005
202-638-2269
www.naacp.org

National Labor Committee
275 Seventh Ave.
15th Floor
New York, NY 10001
212-242-3002
www.nlcnet.org

National Organization for Women
P.O. Box 96824
Washington, DC 20090–6824
202-331-0066
www.now.org/

New Party
88 Third Ave.
Suite 313
Brooklyn, NY 11217
800-200-1294
www.newparty.org/

Oxfam America
26 West St.
Boston, MA 02111
800-77-OXFAM
www.oxfamamerica.org/

Peoples' Global Action against
  'Free' Trade and the WTO
www.agp.org

Webactive
www.webactive.com

Witness for Peace
1229 Fifteenth St., NW
Washington, DC 20005
202-588-1471
www.w4peace.org

In addition, Web sites for such groups as the following may be found easily through standard search engines: Greenpeace; Independent Media Center; 50 Years Is Enough: U.S. Network for Global Economic Justice; The Ruckus Society; Action Resource Center; Act UP.

WORKS CITED

Abrahams, Peter. 1989. *Mine Boy*. Portsmouth, N.Y.: Heinemann.

Achebe, Chinua. 1959. *Things Fall Apart: The Story of a Strong Man*. New York: Astor-Honor.

Adams, Henry, Lester Wright, and Bethany Lohr. 1996. Is Homophobia Associated with Homosexual Arousal? *Journal of Abnormal Psychology* 105, no. 3: 440–45.

American Psychological Association. n.d. Sexual Harassment: Myths and Realities. Http: //www.apa.org/pubinfo/harass.html.

Amnesty International. 1996a. USA: New York Police Shooting Highlights Need for Inquiry. Http://www.oil.ca/amnesty/news/1996/25105896.html.

———. 1996b. USA: Police Brutality Widespread Problem in New York City. 27 June. Http: //www.oil.ca/amnesty/news/1996/25105096.html.

———. 1999a. USA: From Alabama to Wyoming: Fifty Counts of Double Standards—the Missing Entries in the U.S. Report on Human Rights. Http://www.amnesty.org/news/1999/25103399.htm.

———. 1999b. USA: Race, Rights, and Police Brutality. Http://www.amnesty.org/news/1999/25115199.htm.

Andersen, Robin. 1991. Gulf War: Media's Top Sports Event. *Guardian* (New York), 6 February, 4.

Anderson, David C. 1995. *Crime and the Politics of Hysteria: How the Willie Horton Story Changed American Justice*. New York: Random House.

Anker, Laura, Peter Seybold, and Michael Schwartz. 1987. The Ties that Bind Business and Government. In *The Structure of Power in America: The Corporate Elite as a Ruling Class*, edited by Michael Schwartz. New York: Holmes and Meyer.

Anscombe, G. E. M. 1981. "On the Grammar of 'Enjoy'." In *Metaphysics and the Philosophy of Mind: Collected Philosophical Papers*. Vol. 2. Minneapolis: University of Minnesota Press.

Anti-Anti-War Coverage = Pro-War Coverage. 1991. *Extra!* 4, no. 3 (May):19.

Aristotle. 1984. *Nicomachean Ethics*. Translated by W. D. Ross. Revised by J. O. Urmson. Vol. 2 of *The Complete Works of Aristotle*, edited by Jonathan Barnes. Princeton, N.J.: Princeton University Press.

Armstrong, Robert, and Janet Shenk. 1982. *El Salvador: The Face of Revolution*. Boston: South End Press.

Atwood, Margaret. 1985. *The Handmaid's Tale.* New York: Fawcett Crest.

Baer, Michael, and Dean Jaros. 1974. Participation as Instrument and Expression: Some Evidence from the States. *American Journal of Political Science* 18, no. 2 (May):365–83.

Balibar, Etienne, and Immanuel Wallerstein. 1991. *Race, Nation, Class: Ambiguous Identities.* Translation of Balibar by Chris Turner. New York: Verso.

Barner-Barry, Carol. 1986. Rob: Children's Use of Peer Ostracism to Control Aggressive Behavior. *Ethology and Sociobiology* 7:281–93.

Batson, C. Daniel, and Christopher Burris. 1994. Personal Religion: Depressant or Stimulant of Prejudice and Discrimination? In *The Psychology of Prejudice: The Ontario Symposium, Volume 7,* edited by Mark Zanna and James Olsen. Hillsdale, N.J.: Lawrence Erlbaum Associates.

Biener, Lois, and Louis Boudreau. 1991. Social Power and Influence. In *Social Psychology,* edited by Reuben M. Baron and William G. Graziano with Charles Stangor. Fort Worth, Tex.: Holt, Rinehart, and Winston.

Blackstock, Nelson. 1975. *Cointelpro: The FBI's Secret War on Political Freedom.* New York: Vintage.

Bleifuss, Joel. 1999. New World Order. *In These Times,* 22 August, 1.

Bourdieu, Pierre. 1984. *Distinction: A Social Critique of the Judgement of Taste.* Translated by Richard Nice. Cambridge, Mass.: Harvard University Press.

Bradsher, Keith. 1996. Rich Control More of U.S. Wealth, Study Says, as Debts Grow for Poor. *New York Times,* 22 June, 31–32.

Brownstein, Ronald, and Nina Easton. 1982. *Reagan's Ruling Class: Portraits of the President's Top 100 Officials.* Washington, D.C.: Presidential Accountability Group.

Bureau of Justice Statistics. n.d. Criminal Offenders Statistics. Http://www.ojp.usdoj.gov/bjs/crimoff.htm.

Buruma, Ian. 1992. Outsiders. *New York Review of Books* 39, no. 7 (9 April):15–16, 18–19.

Bush, George. 1991. Transcript of the Comments by Bush on the Air Strikes against the Iraqis. *New York Times,* 17 January, A14.

Calder, Lendol. 1999. *Financing the American Dream: A Cultural History of Consumer Credit.* Princeton, N.J.: Princeton University Press.

Callinicos, Luli. 1981. *A People's History of South Africa (Volume Two): Working Life, 1886–1940.* Johannesburg: Ravan Press.

Casualties at Home: Muzzled Journalists. 1991. *Extra!* 4, no. 3 (May):15.

Center on Budget and Policy Priorities. 1998. Poverty Rates Fall, but Remain High for a Period with Such Low Unemployment. Http://www.cbpp.org/9-24-98pov.htm.

Chalmers, David M. 1981. *Hooded Americanism: The History of the Ku Klux Klan.* 2d ed. New York: New Viewpoints.

Chodorow, Nancy. *The Reproduction of Mothering.* Berkeley: U of California P, 1978.

Chomsky, Noam. 1987. Introduction to *The Reagan Administration and Nicaragua,* by Morris Morley and James Petras. New York: Institute for Media Analysis.

——. 1991. Twentieth Century American Propaganda. *Propaganda Review* 8 (fall):38.

——. 1995. *Powers and Prospects: Reflections on Human Nature and the Social Order.* Boston: South End Press.

Clark, Ramsey. 1992. *The Fire This Time: U.S. War Crimes in the Gulf.* New York: Thunder's Mouth Press.

Cleared by Self-Censors? 1991. *Extra!* 4, no. 3 (May):15.

Cockburn, Alexander. 1992. Beat the Devil. *Nation,* 27 January, 78.

Cohen, Dan, and Joe Lauria. 1991. In New Mexico You Can Hit an Anti-War Protester with Impunity. *Guardian* (New York), 3 July, 6.

Cohen, Joshua, and Joel Rogers. 1983. *On Democracy: Toward a Transformation of American Society.* New York: Penguin Books.

Colhoun, Jack. 1991. High-Tech Weapons Star in D.C. Parade. *Guardian* (New York), 19 June, 4.

Crocker, Jennifer, and Brenda Major. 1994. Reactions to Stigma: The Moderating Role of Justifications. In *The Psychology of Prejudice: The Ontario Symposium, Volume 7,* edited by Mark Zanna and James Olsen. Hillsdale, N.J.: Lawrence Erlbaum Associates.

Crompton, Louis. 1985. *Byron and Greek Love: Homophobia in Nineteenth-Century England.* Berkeley: University of California Press.

Crossette, Barbara. 1995. Iraq Sanctions Kill Children, U.N. Reports. *New York Times,* 1 December, A9.

———. 1996. U.N. Survey Finds World Rich-Poor Gap Widening. *New York Times,* 15 July, A3.

Currie, Elliott. 1998. *Crime and Punishment in America.* New York: Henry Holt.

Curtis, L. Perry. 1968. *Anglo-Saxons and Celts: A Study of Anti-Irish Prejudice in Victorian England.* Bridgeport, Conn.: Conference on British Studies, University of Bridgeport.

———. 1971. *Apes and Angels: The Irishman in Victorian Caricature.* Washington, D.C.: Smithsonian Institution Press.

Davey, Joseph Dillon. 1998. *The Politics of Prison Expansion: Winning Elections by Waging War on Crime.* Westport, Conn.: Praeger.

Davis, Mark H. 1994. *Empathy: A Social Psychological Approach.* Madison, Wis.: Brown and Benchmark.

Defund Corporate Welfare. 1997. *Progressive* (March):10.

de Gobineau, Arthur. 1856. *The Moral and Intellectual Diversity of Races.* Intro. H. Hotz. Philadelphia: J. B. Lippincott.

Demeter, John. 1991. Boston Cracks Down on Anti-War Activists. *Guardian* (New York), 27 February, 3.

Dib, Mohammed. 1952. *La grande maison.* Paris: Editions du Seuil.

Dovidio, John, and Samuel Gaertner, eds. 1986. *Prejudice, Discrimination, and Racism.* New York: Academic Press.

Douglas, Susan. 1996. Human Nature and the Newsroom. *Progressive* (July):17.

———. 1997a. Masks and Ratings. *Progressive* (March):19.

———. 1997b. Body-Bag Journalism. *Progressive* (April):19.

Draper, Theodore. 1992. The True History of the Gulf War. *New York Review of Books* 39, no. 3 (30 January): 40.

Duckitt, John H. 1992. *The Social Psychology of Prejudice.* New York: Praeger.

Epstein, Cynthia Fuchs. 1988. *Deceptive Distinctions: Sex, Gender, and the Social Order.* New Haven, Conn.: Yale University Press.

Essed, Philomena. 1991. *Understanding Everyday Racism: An Interdisciplinary Theory.* Newbury Park, Calif.: Sage Publications.

Esses, Victoria, Geoffrey Haddock, and Mark Zanna. 1994. The Role of Mood in the Expression of Intergroup Stereotypes. In *The Psychology of Prejudice: The Ontario Symposium, Volume 7,* edited by Mark Zanna and James Olsen. Hillsdale, N.J.: Lawrence Erlbaum Associates.

"Everyone's Rich in Media-Land . . . But You?" 1999. *Extra! Update.* August, 4.

Fajnzylber, Pablo, Daniel Lederman, and Norman Loayza. 1998. *Determinants of Crime Rates in Latin America and the World: An Empirical Assessment.* Washington, D.C.: World Bank.

Faludi, Susan. 1991. *Backlash: The Undeclared War against American Women.* New York: Crown.

Fanon, Frantz. 1967. *Black Skin, White Masks.* Translated by Charles Lam Markmann. New York: Grove Press.

Faust, David. 1984. *The Limits of Scientific Reasoning.* Minneapolis: University of Minnesota Press.

Fausto-Sterling, Anne. 1985. *Myths of Gender: Biological Theories about Women and Men.* New York: Basic Books.

Frank, Robert H. 1999. *Luxury Fever: Why Money Fails to Satisfy in an Era of Excess.* New York: Free Press.

Fraser, Steven, ed. 1995. *The Bell Curve Wars: Race, Intelligence, and the Future of America.* New York: Basic Books.

Freud, Anna. 1966. *The Ego and the Mechanisms of Defense.* Rev. ed. New York: International Universities Press.

Fuentes, Annette. 1997. Hidden Injuries of NAFTA. *In These Times,* 14 April, 6–7.

Full Court Press. 1991. *Nation,* 11 February, 145.

Gallup, George, Jr. 1992. *The Gallup Poll: Public Opinion 1992.* Wilmington, Del.: Scholarly Resources.

Gerbrands, A. A. 1978. The Anthropological Approach. In *Main Trends in Aesthetics and the Sciences of Art,* edited by Mikel Dufrenne. New York: Holmes and Meier.

Gilman, Sander. 1985. Black Bodies, White Bodies: Toward an Iconography of Female Sexuality in Late-Nineteenth-Century Art, Medicine, and Literature. *Critical Inquiry* 12, no. 1:204–42.

——. 1991. *The Jew's Body.* New York: Routledge.

Gitlin, Todd. 1995. *The Twilight of Common Dreams: Why America Is Wracked by Culture Wars.* New York: Metropolitan Books.

Gleason, Jean Berko. 1987. Sex Differences in Parent-Child Interaction. In *Language, Gender, and Sex in Comparative Perspective,* edited by Susan Philips, Susan Steele, and Christine Tanz. Cambridge, U.K.: Cambridge University Press.

Gould, Stephen Jay. 1981. *The Mismeasure of Man.* New York: W. W. Norton.

Green and Unpleasant Land. 1988. *New Republic* 198, 11 April, 7–9.

Gross, Samuel R., and Robert Mauro. 1989. *Death and Discrimination: Racial Disparities in Capital Sentencing.* Boston: Northeastern University Press.

Guyer, Jocelyn, and Cindy Mann. 1999. Employed but Not Insured. Washington, D.C.: Center on Budget and Policy Priorities. Http://www.cbpp.org/2-9-99mcaid.htm.

Hair, Penda. 1996. Color-Blind—Or Just Blind? *Nation,* 14 October, 12, 14.

Halliday, Denis. 1999. Dennis Halliday. Interviewed by Matthew Rothschild. *Progressive*, February, 26–29.

Hamilton, David, and Tina Trolier. 1986. Stereotypes and Stereotyping: An Overview of the Cognitive Approach. In *Prejudice, Discrimination, and Racism*, edited by John Dovidio and Samuel Gaertner. New York: Academic Press.

Hay, Douglas. 1995. Time, Inequality, and Law's Violence. In *Law's Violence*, edited by Austin Sarat and Thomas R. Kearns. Ann Arbor: University of Michigan Press.

Hayden, Tom, and Connie Rice. 1995. The Future for Education: California Cracks Its Mortarboards. *Nation*, 18 September, 264–66.

Heinze, Eric. 1995. *Sexual Orientation: A Human Right*. Dordrecht, Netherlands: Martinus Nijhoff.

Herman, Edward, and Noam Chomsky. 1988. *Manufacturing Consent: The Political Economy of the Mass Media*. New York: Pantheon Books.

Hirschfeld, Lawrence A. 1996. *Race in the Making: Cognition, Culture, and the Child's Construction of Human Kinds*. Cambridge, Mass.: MIT Press.

Hitler, Adolf. 1940. *Mein Kampf*. Ed. and trans. John Chamberlain et al. New York: Reynal and Hitchcock.

Hogan, Patrick Colm. 1990. *The Politics of Interpretation: Ideology, Professionalism, and the Study of Literature*. New York: Oxford University Press.

———. 1992–1993. Paternalism, Ideology, and Ideological Critique: Teaching *Cry, the Beloved Country*. *College Literature* 19/20, nos. 3/1 (October/February):206–10.

———. 1993. Teaching and Research as Economic Problems. *Education and Society* 11, no. 1:15–25.

———. 1998. On Reading Law as Literature. *College Literature* 25, no. 1:231–36.

Holland, J., et al. 1987. *Induction: Processes of Inference, Learning, and Discovery*. Cambridge, Mass.: MIT Press.

Holmes, Colin. 1989. "Alexander Ratcliffe, Militant Protestant and Antisemite." In *Traditions of Intolerance: Historical Perspectives on Fascism and Race Discourse in Britain*, edited by Tony Kushner and Kenneth Lunn. Manchester, U.K.: Manchester University Press: 196–217.

Horrobin, David. 1982. Peer Review: A Philosophically Faulty Concept Which Is Proving Disastrous for Science. *Behavioral and Brain Sciences* 5, no. 2:217–18.

Houppert, Karne. 1999. You're Not Entitled! Welfare "Reform" Is Leading to Government Lawlessness. *Nation*, 25 October, 11–18.

Hudson, R. A. 1980. *Sociolinguistics*. Cambridge, U.K.: Cambridge University Press.

Isichei, Elizabeth. 1976. *A History of the Igbo People*. New York: St. Martin's Press.

Ivins, Molly. 1999. Heavy Money Floats to the Top. *News and Observer* (Raleigh, N.C.), 5 September.

Jenkins, Peter. 1988. Odd Man Out. *New York Review of Books* 35 (21 July):9–11.

Jenkins, William D. 1990. *Steel Valley Klan: The Ku Klux Klan in Ohio's Mahoning Valley*. Kent, Ohio: Kent State University Press.

Jhally, Sut, Justin Lewis, and Michael Morgan. 1991. The Gulf War: A Study of the Media, Public Opinion, and Public Knowledge. *Propaganda Review* 8 (fall): 50–52.

Johnson-Laird, P. N., and P. C. Watson, eds. 1977. *Thinking: Readings in Cognitive Science*. Cambridge, U.K.: Cambridge University Press.

Johnston, David Cay. 1999. Gap between Rich and Poor Found Substantially Wider. *New York Times*, 5 September, 16.

Jolly, Richard, et al. 1999. *Globalization with a Human Face: Human Development Report 1999*. London: United Nations Development Program.

Kaidy, Mitchell. 1991. War Brings Anti-Arab Racists out of the Woodwork. *Guardian* (New York), 30 January, 18.

Kaltenheuser, Skip. 1997. King of the Hill. *Barron's*, 13 January, 56–57.

Klementz-Belgardt, Edith. 1981. American Research on Response to Literature: The Empirical Studies. *Poetics* 10:357–80.

Kluger, Richard. 1996. *Ashes to Ashes: America's Hundred-Year Cigarette War, the Public Health, and the Unabashed Triumph of Philip Morris*. New York: Alfred A. Knopf.

Kraft, Stephanie. 1991. It Can't Happen Here (Or Can It?). *Hartford Advocate*, 7 March, 11.

Krinsky, Robert. 1991. Peace Ads Shut out of Debate. *Extra!* 4, no. 3 (May):18.

Kushner, Tony. 1989. *The Persistence of Prejudice: Antisemitism in British Society during the Second World War*. Manchester, U.K.: Manchester University Press.

Labor Party. n.d. A Call for Economic Justice. Http://www.labornet.org/lpa/documents/program.htm.

Lakoff, George. 1991a. The Arab Viewpoint. *Propaganda Review* 8 (fall):58.

——. 1991b. Metaphors of War. *Propaganda Review* 8 (fall):18.

Lakoff, George, and Mark Johnson. 1980. *Metaphors We Live By*. Chicago: University of Chicago Press.

Lakoff, George, and Mark Turner. 1989. *More than Cool Reason: A Field Guide to Poetic Metaphor*. Chicago: University of Chicago Press.

Langlois, J. H., and L. A. Roggman. 1990. "Attractive Faces Are Only Average." *Psychological Science* 1:115–21.

Lapping, Brian. 1989. *Apartheid: A History*. Rev. ed. New York: George Braziller.

Lembcke, Jerry. 1991. Vietnam Veterans Were Welcomed into Radical Fold. *Hartford Courant*, 17 February, D1, D4.

Lessing, Doris. 1964. *A Proper Marriage*. New York: New American Library.

——. 1976. *The Grass Is Singing*. New York: New American Library.

Levy, Clifford. 1996. A Racial Study Finds Differences in Jail Sentences. *New York Times*, 10 April, B1.

Loftus, Elizabeth. 1980. *Memory*. Reading, Mass.: Addison-Wesley.

Lowe, Ben. 1991. Arabs Face Detention, Deportation in Europe. *Guardian* (New York), 6 February, 14.

Mahoney, Michael. 1977. Publication Prejudices: An Experimental Study of Confirmatory Bias in the Peer Review System. *Cognitive Therapy and Research* 1:161–75.

Males, Mike. 1994. Bashing Youth: Media Myths about Teenagers. *Extra!* 7, no. 2 (March/April):8–11.

Males, Mike, and Faye Docuyanan. 1996. Crackdown on Kids: Giving up on the Young. *Progressive* (February):24–26.

Mann, Thomas. Forthcoming. The U.S. Campaign Finance System under Strain. In *Setting National Priorities: The 2000 Election and Beyond*. Washington, D.C.: Brookings Press.

Marx, Karl. 1967. *Capital (Volume 1): A Critical Analysis of Capitalist Production.* Edited by Friedrich Engels. Translated by Samuel Moore and Edward Aveling. New York: International Publishers.

———. 1975. Critique of Hegel's Philosophy of Right: Introduction. In *Early Writings,* translated by Rodney Livingstone and Gregor Benton. New York: Vintage.

Mason, J. W. 1996. The Gulag Society. *In These Times,* 19 August, 34–36.

McChesney, Robert W. 1999. *Rich Media, Poor Democracy: Communication Politics in Dubious Times.* Urbana: University of Illinois Press.

McCuen, Gary. 1974. *The Racist Reader: Analyzing Primary Source Readings by American Race Supremacists.* Anoka, Minn.: Greenhaven Press.

McEnroe, Colin. 1991. War of the Words. *Hartford Courant,* 19 February, B1.

McManus, John H. 1994. *Market-Driven Journalism: Let the Citizen Beware?* Thousand Oaks, Calif.: Sage.

Media Rewrites UN History. 1991. *Extra!* 4, no. 3 (May):22.

Mill, John Stuart. 1971. On Liberty. In *Essential Works of John Stuart Mill,* edited by Max Lerner. New York: Bantam.

Milton, John. 1932. The Reason of Church Government Urged against Prelaty. In *The Works of John Milton,* edited by Frank Patterson et al. New York: Columbia University Press.

Mokhiber, Russell. 1996. Underworld, U.S.A. *In These Times,* 1 April, 14–16.

Muwakkil, Salim. 1997. Getting Away with Murder. *In These Times,* 6 January, 16–18.

Mynatt, Clifford, Michael Doherty, and Ryan Tweney. 1977. Confirmation Bias in a Simulated Research Environment: An Experimental Study of Scientific Inference. In *Thinking: Readings in Cognitive Science,* edited by P. N. Johnson-Laird and P. C. Watson. Cambridge, U.K.: Cambridge University Press.

Nader, Ralph. 1982. Introduction to *Reagan's Ruling Class: Portraits of the President's Top 100 Officials,* by Ronald Brownstein and Nina Easton. Washington, D.C.: Presidential Accountability Group.

Naked Cities. 1997. *Nation,* 6 January, 3–4.

Nandy, Ashis. 1983. *The Intimate Enemy: Loss and Recovery of Self under Colonialism.* Delhi: Oxford University Press.

———. 1987. *Traditions, Tyranny, and Utopias: Essays in the Politics of Awareness.* Delhi: Oxford University Press.

Naureckas, Jim. 1991. Gulf War Coverage: The Worst Censorship Was at Home. *Extra!* 4, no. 3 (May 1991): 3–10.

Neier, Aryeh. 1991. Watching Rights. *Nation,* 11 March, 295.

Neuberg, Steven. 1994. Expectancy-Confirmation Processes in Stereotype-Tinged Social Encounters: The Moderating Role of Social Goals. In *The Psychology of Prejudice: The Ontario Symposium, Volume 7,* edited by Mark Zanna and James Olsen. Hillsdale, N.J.: Lawrence Erlbaum Associates.

Nickerson, Stephanie, Clara Mayo, and Althea Smith. 1986. Racism in the Courtroom. In *Prejudice, Discrimination, and Racism,* edited by John Dovidio and Samuel Gaertner. New York: Academic Press.

Nisbett, Richard E., and Lee Ross. 1980. *Human Inference: Strategies and Shortcomings of Social Judgment*. Englewood Cliffs, N.J.: Prentice-Hall.

Noble, Kenneth. 1996. Race Issue Rattles Celebrity Haven. *New York Times*, 23 April, A14.

Novick, Michael. 1991. War Fallout: Attacks on Arabs and Jews. *Guardian* (New York), 6 February, 5.

Nussbaum, Martha C. 1986. *The Fragility of Goodness: Luck and Ethics in Greek Tragedy and Philosophy*. Cambridge, U.K.: Cambridge University Press.

Ogden, Don. 1991. Wimps of War Get Nasty. *Guardian* (New York), 13 February, 7.

One in Seven. 1997. *Nation*, 24 February, 7.

Ortony, Andrew, Gerald Clore, and Allan Collins. 1988. *The Cognitive Structure of Emotions*. New York: Cambridge University Press.

Pagels, Elaine. 1995. *The Origin of Satan*. New York: Vintage.

Parenti, Christian. 1999. SWAT Nation. *Nation*, 31 May, 16–21.

Parrott, Sharon. 1998. *Welfare Recipients Who Find Jobs: What Do We Know about Their Employment and Earnings?* Washington, D.C.: Center on Budget and Policy Priorities.

Passell, Peter. 1994. Economic Scene. *New York Times*, 27 January, D2.

Paton, Alan. 1987. *Cry, the Beloved Country*. New York: Collier Books.

Peukert, Detlev. 1982. *Inside Nazi Germany: Conformity, Opposition, and Racism in Everyday Life*. Translated by Richard Deveson. New Haven: Yale University Press.

Plant, Richard. 1986. *The Pink Triangle: The Nazi War against Homosexuals*. New York: Henry Holt.

"Polling Game, The." 1991. *Extra!* 4, no. 3 (May):11.

Pollitt, Katha. 1995. Hers. *New York Times*, 12 December, C2.

A Promising Victory for the Poor. 1997. *New York Times*, 7 January, A16.

Primus, Wendell, et al. 1999. *The Initial Impacts of Welfare Reform on the Incomes of Single-Mother Families*. Washington, D.C.: Center on Budget and Policy Priorities.

Purchase, Graham. 1996. *Evolution and Revolution: An Introduction to the Life and Thought of Peter Kropotkin*. Sydney, Australia: Jura Media.

Putnam, Hilary. 1975. "The Meaning of 'Meaning.' " In *Mind, Language, and Reality: Philosophical Papers, Volume 2*. Cambridge: Cambridge University Press, 215–71.

Rallies for Troops Stir Quiet Majority. 1991. *Hartford Courant*, 11 February, A6.

Rasmussen, Chris. 1999. Debt Wish. *In These Times*, 31 October, 19–20.

Redfield, Robert. 1953. Primitive World View. In *The Primitive World and Its Transformations*, edited by Robert Redfield. Ithaca, N.Y.: Cornell University Press.

Reeves, Frank. 1983. *British Racial Discourse: A Study of British Political Discourse about Race and Race-Related Matters*. Cambridge, U.K.: Cambridge University Press.

Rich, Frank. 1995. The Gloved Ones. *New York Times*, 18 June, sec. 4, 15.

Rich, Melissa, and Thomas Cash. 1993. The American Image of Beauty: Media Representations of Hair Color for Four Decades. *Sex-Roles* 29, nos. 1–2:113–24.

Rodney, Walter. 1972. *How Europe Underdeveloped Africa*. Washington, D.C.: Howard University Press.

Ross, Lee, and Richard E. Nisbett. 1991. *The Person and the Situation: Perspectives of Social Psychology*. Philadelphia, Pa.: Temple University Press.

Rushdie, Salman. 1989. *Shame*. New York: Vintage.

Russell, Katheryn K. 1998. *The Color of Crime*. New York: New York University Press.

Said, Edward. 1978. *Orientalism*. New York: Pantheon.

Sarkar, Sumit. 1973. *The Swadeshi Movement in Bengal, 1903–1908*. New Delhi: People's Publishing House.

Schiller, Friedrich. 1954. *On the Aesthetic Education of Man in a Series of Letters*. Translated by Reginald Snell. London: Routledge and Kegan Paul.

Schor, Juliet. 1991. *The Overworked American: The Unexpected Decline of Leisure*. New York: Basic Books.

Schwartz, Michael, ed. 1987. *The Structure of Power in America: The Corporate Elite as a Ruling Class*. New York: Holmes and Meyer.

Schwartz, Norbert. 1995. Social Cognition: Information Accessibility and Use in Social Judgment. In *Thinking: An Invitation to Cognitive Science (Volume 3)*, edited by Edward E. Smith and Daniel N. Osherson. 2d ed. Cambridge, Mass.: MIT Press.

Shapiro, Bruce. 1997. Sleeping Lawyer Syndrome. *Nation*, 7 April, 27–29.

Shapiro, Isaac, and Robert Greenstein. 1999. *The Widening Income Gulf*. Washington, D.C.: Center on Budget and Policy Priorities.

Simons, H. J., and R. E. Simons. 1969. *Class and Colour in South Africa: 1850–1950*. Baltimore, Md.: Penguin.

Sklar, Holly. 1991. Buried Stories from Media Gulf. *Z Magazine* (March):57–61.

Smith, Jonathan Z. 1985. What a Difference a Difference Makes. In *To See Ourselves as Others See Us: Christians, Jews, "Others" in Late Antiquity*, edited by Jacob Neusner and Ernest Frerichs. Chico, Calif.: Scholars Press.

Socioeconomic Status and Health Chartbook in Health, United States, 1998. 1998. Http://www.cdc.gov/nchswww/products/pubs/pubd/hus/2010/98chtbk.htm.

Soloman, Norman. 1991. War Deaths Mere PR to Media's Eyes. *Guardian* (New York), 27 February, 4.

Spin Control through Censorship: The Pentagon Manages the News. 1991. *Extra!* 4, no. 3 (May):14.

Stephens, Beth. 1991. FBI's Probe Feeds Hysteria about Terrorism. *Guardian* (New York), 13 February, 5.

Tversky, Amos, and Daniel Kahneman. 1977. Judgment under Uncertainty: Heuristics and Biases. In *Thinking: Readings in Cognitive Science*, edited by P. N. Johnson-Laird and P. C. Watson. Cambridge, U.K.: Cambridge University Press.

Unequal Sentencing. 1996. *New York Times*, 15 April, A14.

USA by Numbers: A Statistical Portrait of the United States. 1988. Washington, D.C.: Zero Population Growth.

U.S. Bureau of the Census. 1991. Poverty in the United States: 1990. *Current Population Reports*. Series P-60, no. 175. Washington, D.C.: Government Printing Office.

———. 1992. Extended Measures of Well-Being: Selected Data from the 1984 Survey of Income and Program Participation. *Current Population Reports*. Series P–70, no. 26. Washington, D.C.: Government Printing Office.

——. 1998. Money Income in the United States: 1997 (with Separate Data on Valuation of Noncash Benefits). *Current Population Reports*. Series P–60, no. 200. Washington, D.C.: Government Printing Office.

——. 1999. Extended Measures of Well-Being: Meeting Basic Needs (1995). *Current Population Reports*. Series P–70, no. 67. Washington, D.C.: Government Printing Office.

U.S. Department of Justice. n.d. Myths Feed Denial about Family Violence. Http://www.usdoj. gov/wawo/manual/myths.html:1.

van Dijk, Teun. 1987. *Communicating Racism: Ethnic Prejudice in Thought and Talk*. Newbury Park, Calif.: Sage Publications.

"Victory in the Desert" Video. 1991. *Propaganda Review* 8, 63.

Voltaire, François-Marie Arouet. 1980. *Candide, or Optimism*. Translated by Robert M. Adams. Vol. 2 of *The Norton Anthology of World Masterpieces*, edited by Maynard Mack et al. 4th continental ed. New York: W. W. Norton.

Weber, Max. 1968. *Economy and Society*. 3 vols. New York: Bedminster Press.

Weir, Fred. 1991. Moscow Jittery over Course of Gulf War. *Guardian* (New York), 6 February, 15.

White, Richard T. 1992. Implications of Recent Research on Learning for Curriculum and Assessment. *Journal of Curriculum Studies* 24, no. 2:153–64.

White House Inhospitality. 1995. *New York Times*, 16 June, A26.

Wilkinson, Richard G. 1990. Income Distribution and Mortality: A "Natural" Experiment. *Sociology of Health and Illness* 12:391–412.

Wills, T. A. 1981. Downward Comparison Principles in Social Psychology. *Psychological Bulletin* 90:245–71.

Wilson's War on the Poor. 1997. *In These Times*, 17 February, 10–11.

Wolff, Edward. 1996. *Top Heavy: The Increasing Inequality of Wealth in America and What Can Be Done about It*. New York: New Press.

Workfare Rights. 1997. *Progressive*, April, 10.

Zippelius, Reinhold. 1986. Exclusion and Shunning as Legal and Social Sanctions. *Ethology and Sociobiology* 7:159–66.

INDEX

Calder, Lendol, 43, 44
Callinicos, Luli, 153, 154
Campaign finance, 7, 8
Capitalism, 1, 9, 22, 24, 40, 43, 46, 47, 62,
  63, 85, 132, 139, 140
Capital punishment, 16, 17, 147, 153
Cash, Thomas, 125
Censorship, 66–70
Chalmers, David M., 26
Chomsky, Noam, 3, 15, 80, 83, 85
Circumcision, 146
Clark, Ramsey, 16, 17
Class action suits, 19–20
Clore, Gerald, 130
Cockburn, Alexander, 23
Coercion: formal, 9, 13–22; informal, 9,
  29–34; internal, 9
Cohen, Dan, 26
Cohen, Joshua, 5, 7, 82
Colhoun, Jack, 102
Collins, Allan, 130
Colonialism, 48, 63–64, 107, 122, 134, 138–
  41
Communist Party of South Africa (CPSA),
  150
Comparison: direct, 100, 101; downward,
  49
Confirmatory bias, 10, 74, 77, 83, 110, 121,
  122, 127
Conformity: imitative, 30, 44, 53, 57
Consent: calculated, 13–58
Conservatism, 15, 39, 83, 131, 134, 154;
  ideological, 141, 144, 148; pragmatic, 141,
  144, 148; revolutionary, 141, 145; roman-
  tic, 141, 145
Constitution of the United States, 15
Consultation: as pacification, 82, 85, 86
Consumer credit, 43
Consumerism, 43, 44, 46
Cooper, James, 142
Corruption: oppressive, 9, 15, 22, 25–28
Crime: corporate, 15, 17–19; metaphor of
  illness for, 131, 145; and poverty, 6; street,
  15–18
Crocker, Jennifer, 51
Crompton, Louis, 147
Crossette, Barbara, 3, 16, 115

Currie, Elliott, 6
Curtis, L. Perry, 55, 143

Darley, J., 52
Davey, Joseph Dillon, 22
Davis, Mark H., 65, 92, 93, 156
Deceit, 67
de Gobineau, Arthur, 141
Dehumanization, 88, 91–96, 115, 131
Demand(s), 40–46, 51, 57; hollow, 44
Demeter, John, 24
Democracy, 1, 7, 13, 59, 62, 72, 85, 107, 132
Dependency, 38–40
Desire, 40–45; false, 40, 43, 44; true, 40
Despair, 79, 81, 82, 87, 92
Diallo, Amadou, 21, 142
Dib, Mohammed, ix
Discourse, 67, 72–74, 84, 105, 150; ellipsis
  in, 72, 73; emphasis in, 72–74; structure
  of, 67, 72–74
Disdain: social, 29–32
Disenfranchisement, 21, 153
Dissent, 1, 2, 8, 11–13, 27, 33, 34, 36, 37,
  45, 47, 58, 77, 81, 104, 108, 109, 135, 136,
  138, 157
Docuyanan, Faye, 137
Doherty, Michael, 74
Domains, 9, 10, 119, 132–48, 155; animacy,
  133, 134, 140–47, 155; maturity, 133–40,
  143
Douglas, Susan, 68, 69, 75, 84, 131
Draper, Theodore, 23
Duckitt, J. H., 49, 54, 64, 96–98, 100, 130,
  131, 136
Dukakis, Michael, 107

Eagly, A. H., 55
Earthy, Patrick, 24
Easton, Nina, 8
Economy, 1–9, 13, 15, 18, 34–47, 53, 84, 86,
  87, 89, 98, 99, 128–30, 139, 140, 143, 153,
  154, 157; growth of, 5, 6; insecurity in,
  34–40, 46, 157
Elections, 7, 37, 85, 86
Emotion, 10, 13, 20, 40, 43, 50, 52, 87, 89,
  92–96, 101–13, 129–31
Empathy, 10, 56, 88, 92–94, 143, 156

tributive sub-directory, 120, 121; personal preferences, 121, 122; prestige, 122, 125; probes, 129; semantic field, 132. *See also* Domains

Liberalism, 15, 106, 107, 134–36, 139, 140, 148, 154; ideological, 135, 136, 148; pragmatic, 135, 136, 148; revolutionary, 135, 139; romantic, 135, 140

Literary theory: non-European, 70

Loayza, Norman, 6

Lohr, Bethany, 31, 118

Lowe, Ben, 23, 24

Luke the Evangelist, 53

Madison, James, 15

Mahoney, Michael, 74, 76, 83

Major, Brenda, 292

Males, Mike, 136, 137

Mann, Cindy, 36

Mann, Thomas, 7

Manufacturing consent, 60

Marriage, 33, 42, 43

Marx, Karl, 63

Marxism, 9, 39, 81, 82, 89, 140, 148

Mary (mother of Jesus), 144

Mason, J. W., 6, 7, 21

Matthew the Evangelist, 53

Mauro, Robert, 142, 153

Mayo, Clara, 20, 143

McCarthy, Eugene, 86

McChesney, Robert W., 7

McCuen, Gary, 142, 146

McEnroe, Colin, 71

McManus, John H., 68, 69

Memory: and bias, 75, 110

Meritocracy, 51, 83

Metabelief(s), 9, 79–82

Metaphor, 70, 71, 102, 132, 145, 149, 150

Microhierarchization, 9, 46–49, 89, 143

Milgram, Stanley, 157

Mill, John Stuart, 30

Milton, John, 137, 144

Models (cognitive): adolescent, 134–38, 142, 148–53; angelic, 133, 140–42, 144, 145; demonic, 140, 141, 144–47; prepubescent, 133–40, 148–54; senile decadent, 135, 138–140, 145; wild animal, 91,

131, 133, 140–44, 147–49, 151, 152, 154; wise elder, 135, 138–40, 144; work animal, 133, 140–44, 147–49, 151, 152, 154

Mohr, Richard, 25, 27

Mokhiber, Russell, 15–18

Monning, Bill, 83–84

Montesquieu, Baron de la Brède et de (Charles Louis de Secondat), 147

Mood, 103, 129–31

Morgan, Michael, 59

Murder, 5, 9, 15–19, 22, 25, 28, 54, 56, 57, 64, 71, 73, 102, 115, 117, 141–44, 146, 148, 149, 151–54. *See also* Killing

Muslims, 48, 89, 92, 105, 111

Muwakkil, Salim, 21, 142

Mynatt, Clifford, 74

Mystification, 38–40; moral, 51, 56, 57

Nader, Ralph, 84

Nandy, Ashis, 134, 136, 138

Narcissism, 10, 87, 88, 102. *See also* Identification

Narcissistic wound, 104

Naureckas, Jim, 24–26, 71–74, 83, 95

Nazi Germany, 23, 56, 60, 127, 145, 147

Need, 40–45; system-internal, 45

Neier, Aryeh, 23

Neuberg, Steven, 74, 75

News reporting, 22, 60, 68–71, 75, 80, 83, 91, 101, 113, 131

Nickerson, Stephanie, 20

Nisbett, Richard, 39, 74, 75, 93, 105, 110, 121

Nixon, Richard, 86

Noble, Kenneth, 24

Northern Ireland, 143

Novick, Michael, 25

Nussbaum, Martha C., 56

Obfuscation, 67, 70, 71, 84

Ogden, Don, 26

Ortony, Andrew, 130

Ostracism, 29–32, 34

Outgroup, 49, 87, 96–100, 109, 115, 128, 130, 132

Overwork, 35, 37, 69

Ownership, 9, 13–15, 133, 153

175

Patrick Colm Hogan is Professor of English and Comparative
Literature at the University of Connecticut. His other books
include: The Politics of Interpretation (1990); Joyce, Milton, and the
Theory of Influence (1995); On Interpretation: Meaning and Inference
in Law, Psychoanalysis, and Literature (1996); Philosophical
Approaches to the Study of Literature (2000); and Colonialism and
Cultural Identity (2000).

Library of Congress Cataloging-in-Publication Data
Hogan, Patrick Colm.
The culture of conformism : understanding social consent /
Patrick Colm Hogan.
Includes bibliographical references and index.
ISBN 0-8223-2705-8 (cloth : alk. paper) —
ISBN 0-8223-2716-3 (pbk. : alk. paper)
1. Conformity. 2. Ideology. I. Title.
HM1246.H64 2001   303.3'2—dc21   00-045184